The
BIG-GAME
FISHING
H A N D B O O K

The
BIG-GAME
FISHING
HANDBOOK

Len Cacutt

FIRST PUBLISHED IN 1999 BY
NEW HOLLAND PUBLISHERS LTD
LONDON • CAPE TOWN • SYDNEY • AUCKLAND

24 NUTFORD PLACE
LONDON W1H 6DQ
UNITED KINGDOM

80 MCKENZIE STREET
CAPE TOWN 8001
SOUTH AFRICA

14 AQUATIC DRIVE
FRENCHS FOREST, NSW 2086
AUSTRALIA

218 LAKE ROAD
NORTHCOTE, AUCKLAND
NEW ZEALAND

ISBN 1 85974 088 X

DESIGNERS: DANIËL JANSEN VAN VUUREN, MICHELLE STAPLES
EDITORS: GILL GORDON, TRACEY HAWTHORNE
PUBLISHING MANAGER: MARIËLLE RENSSEN
ILLUSTRATORS: ANTON KRUGEL, DANIËL JANSEN VAN VUUREN
PICTURE RESEARCHER: CARMEN WATTS
INTERNATIONAL CONSULTANTS:
STEVE COOPER (AUSTRALIA), NIC DE KOCK (SOUTH AFRICA)
CHRIS DAWN (UK AND EUROPE), JIM HARDIE (USA)

REPRODUCTION BY UNIFOTO (PTY) LTD
PRINTED AND BOUND IN SINGAPORE BY TIEN WAH PRESS (PTE) LTD
2 4 6 8 10 9 7 5 3 1

DEDICATION

THE AUTHOR ONCE HAD THE PRIVILEGE OF EDITING, UPDATING AND LARGELY REWRITING A DETAILED COMMENTARY ON A FISHING BOOK WRITTEN BY A WELL-KNOWN AND POPULAR WRITER OF THE 1950S, ERIC MARSHALL HARDY, WHOSE MANY BOOKS WERE EAGERLY READ FOR THEIR FISHING WISDOM. SURELY, HE HAD DONE IT ALL, CAUGHT THEM ALL, FISHED ALL THE SEAS, RIVERS AND STREAMS, USED ALL THE TECHNIQUES? BUT IN HIS INTRODUCTIONS HARDY ALWAYS INSISTED THAT HE WAS THE SPORT'S PR MAN, THAT NO SINGLE ANGLER WOULD HAVE THE TIME TO DO IT ALL, CATCH THEM ALL, FISH ALL THE RIVERS AND SEAS. HE NEVER CLAIMED A COMPLETE WORKING KNOWLEDGE OF ALL THE STYLES AND TECHNIQUES HE DISCUSSED SO ELOQUENTLY, INSISTING THAT HE GATHERED FACTS, FIGURES AND ANSWERS TO PROBLEMS AND PRESENTED THEM IN AN INTERESTING AND READABLE FASHION. THIS VOLUME THEN, SETS OUT TO DO FOR BIG-GAME FISHING TODAY WHAT ERIC MARSHALL HARDY DID FOR HIS READERS 40 AND MORE YEARS AGO.

— LEN CACUTT

FOREWORD

The first fish I ever caught made me feel things I'd never felt before. At the age of five and a half, I experienced a heart-pounding, palm-sweating, knee-trembling adrenaline rush that I can still taste in my mouth today. During a family holiday, I hooked and landed a wrasse off a stone jetty on the west coast of Scotland. Not a big wrasse. Not a record-breaking wrasse, or even a photo-in-the-local-paper wrasse. But a wrasse, which proceeded to pick up a huge stone chisel and carve 'angler' indelibly into the bedrock of my pysche. From that windy day, with green scales on my fingers and a new bend in my inexpensive rod, I went on to devote hideous amounts of time, travel, money, energy, sleep, dreams and fantasies to fishing. To some anglers, fish cease to be fish, in the sense of being simple aquatic creatures. They somehow evolve into a complex collection of emotional responses. Simply the act of catching, or not catching, a fish can invoke a huge range of emotions, from intense pleasure, happiness and peace to disappointment, greed and jealousy.

I've been disgustingly lucky in my fishing life. I've been able to fish on opposite sides of the world. I've travelled two hundred miles deep into the Pacific Ocean, way off the northernmost tip of New Zealand, to troll through azure blue seas chasing unspeakably beautiful, sleek, silver-flanked blue marlin. And then I've come home to fish the dank, dark, silty waters of the Hertford Union canal at the bottom of my garden in east London. In one week I caught an 85-pound sailfish off the Caribbean island of St Lucia and a four-pound bream out of a canal in Hackney. One came out looking like it was brand-new and chromium-plated, leaping from a technicolour sea into a perfect cloudless blue sky. The other was bullied past sunken shopping trolleys, dragged through water the colour of stewed tea, beneath a smog-filled sky scarred with grim tower blocks. Two of the most diverse locations, one obviously beautiful, the other apparently ugly. But strangely enough, the pleasure received wasn't that different. In many ways, I was prouder of that hard-earned inner-city bream than I was of the gorgeous Caribbean beauty.

Len Cacutt's *Big-game Fishing Handbook* takes you on a journey of photographs and text that, even with the experience of fishing around the globe, I can only droolingly dream of. For anyone even remotely harbouring an ambition to one day hire a charterboat to target marlin, or even for those who already have a working knowledge of big-game tactics, this is an essential book. It is a window onto a world of deep sea opportunity, which could bring a warm glow to the darkest, coldest winter night. It's an aspiration and an inspiration.

Probably the greatest thing about big-game fishing is its accessibility. Even if you don't consider yourself a proficient angler you can still experience the sport at its formula one, premier league level. Big-game boats the world over are equipped to cater for the initiated and the totally uninitiated, the expert and the beginner. If you charter the right skipper, on the right day, in the right water, you could find yourself lucky enough to be attached to a big, angry black marlin, tipping the scales at ten times your own body weight, with all the manners of a steroid-pumping Doberman. The joy of game fishing is that it can be blissfully indiscriminate. A complete novice could inadvertently find himself on the business-end of the world's most acrobatic and hardest-fighting fish – a sensation which is like a learner-driver suddenly finding himself behind the wheel of a racing Ferrari, with his foot pushed flat to the floor. And believe me, that is one adrenaline rush from which you can never recover.

NICK FISHER
Writer and presenter of the angling series Screaming Reels *for Channel 4 Television (UK).*

CONTENTS

CHAPTER ONE

A BRIEF HISTORY

In museums of anthropology all over the world there are artefacts of early man. Among them are fish-hooks chipped out of flint or crudely fashioned from deer antler. It is intriguing to wonder what primitive mind-set first produced such a shape, or what motivated early man to conceive the first fish-hook. Perhaps it was a familiarity with insect spines and their propensity to lodge in human or animal skin; or small curved bones (known from the Middle East and dating back to 5000 BC) that gave rise to that first item of fishing tackle; perhaps it was an oddly shaped spearhead that held a struggling fish more securely than a straight point. For fishing purposes, the spear would become known as the harpoon (from the Old Norse *harpa*, to squeeze).

We shall never know, because before man developed the brain power, the ability or the vocabulary, he could not record his thought processes for posterity. It is only when he came to write down his thoughts in pictograms, hieroglyphics and, later, impressing on stone, clay, papyrus and paper recognizable words (to modern eyes and brains), that he was able to communicate something of what was going on in his mind.

There may be clues to man's early fishing habits in certain Neolithic Scandinavian rock carvings, which appear to show an anchored boat and two men with long hooked poles. We know that fishing is an ancient activity. As soon as men began to record events in pictures or words, we see evidence in Assyrian temple carvings of fishermen using hand-lines, of Pharaonic Egyptians in 2000 BC standing on reed boats and using fishing rods with the line attached to the tip, and in eyed hooks, dating to 1500 BC, recovered from Mycenae.

Before Vesuvius overwhelmed them with its lethal and fiery eruption in August AD 79, the inhabitants of the pleasant Roman town of Pompeii used to visit their neighbours in Herculaneum to do some sea fishing, as hooks of a size that could only be used at

This scene, from an ancient Egyptian tomb, shows men using boats and nets to catch a variety of fish.

A medieval angler using a rod, line and float.

sea were found when 19th-century antiquarians began tunnelling through the compacted volcanic ash into the remarkably preserved remains.

The Romans had a liking for fish dishes and used a strongly flavoured, and expensive, fish sauce, called *garum* or *liquamen* by the Roman poet Ovid, on many items of food.

From the ancient classical civilizations through to the Christian era, fishing was both a pastime and a food-gathering necessity. In the fourth century, a Roman poet, Ausonius, who lived in Gaul, described an angler fishing along the Moselle with a horse-hair line and feather lure.

The Chinese *Book of Odes*, written in the seventh century, alluded to more than just fishing, using symbolism about 'long, tapering rods being angled in limpid waters'.

During the period known as the Dark Ages, Europe produced very few books, so it is not surprising that little was written about fishing, although it continued to be an important aspect of food gathering, as well as a source of recreation and pleasure.

A selection of vintage centre-pin reels, together with early models of the multiplier reels generally used today.

Every angler has his set of tales to tell. This book is an angling classic.

Given the relatively primitive nature of fishing tackle at that stage (compared with today's equipment), it is unlikely that the large and powerful species we know collectively as the big-game fishes were deliberately sought, because there would have been little chance of boating or beaching them. What use would there be in putting a small fish on a hook and offering it to a marlin when, even if the marlin were to take the bait, there would be no chance of winning what would certainly be a long, drawn-out struggle?

Sadly, sea angling does not have its Izaak Walton, the philosopher/angler whose *The Compleat Angler* (1653) has ever since been regarded with veneration. However, there were medieval books about angling, such as the *Boke of St Albans*, written by Dame Juliana Berners in 1496, which brought knowledge of the sport to the fore. Angling writers of the 17th and 18th centuries, such as Richard Brookes, were more familiar with the fish than with the tackle that was available at the time. Their knowledge was gained from commercial fishermen who, using nets and long lines, took their lives in their hands every time they left harbour with nothing but their sails to rely on.

Even as late as the mid-19th century, rods for sea fishing were made from rigid, heavy greenheart wood or thick, unyielding bamboo.

Reels of a sort were employed in the recovery of hand-lines carrying a series of baited hooks, which were let down to the seabed to catch mackerel and small food-fish.

Early sea fishing books devoted much space to descriptions of fish and there is ample evidence that this information was often cribbed from textbooks such as ichthyologist William Yarrell's *British Fishes,* first published in 1836.

Unlike the well-documented history of freshwater fishing (especially for trout and salmon), angling for large and powerful fish species from boats in deep salt water did not become an organized branch of sea angling until the mid-19th century.

Although returning whalers spoke in awe of huge marlin, tuna, sharks, sailfish and swordfish they had encountered while at sea, it was not thought possible that these fish could be caught on rod and line. No doubt spearing and harpooning were carried out by commercial fisherman, but little was written about sea fishing as a sport.

Of all the books – good and bad – written about deep-sea game fishing, it must be Zane Grey's that best capture the romance, excitement, escapism and adventure of this kind of fishing.

Born in Zanesville, Ohio, in 1871, Grey trained to become a dentist, but when fishing 'hooked' him he swapped his interest in dentistry for a passion for dentex (a medium-sized food-fish). Grey travelled widely and the money he earned by writing about his numerous fishing expeditions enabled him to enjoy both sea- and fresh-water fishing.

The following paragraph, describing Zane Grey's sighting of a porpoise, is from a slim volume entitled *Tales From a Fisherman's Log*, and was written after a trip out for marlin:

'The rain fell harder, the ship drove on into a roughening sea, the wind grew stronger, the weird light sent a sheen over the water. And I leaned there over the rail, fascinated, watching one of the marvels of nature, perhaps that of the greatest beauty combined with the cruelty and mystery of the deep.'

Grey, who first fell in love with tarpon fishing and then with the big-game fish he encountered in the seas off Australasia (he landed a 319kg, or 704 lb, marlin off New Zealand's Cavalli Islands in 1927), declared in his 1937 work *An American Angler in Australia* that, 'Australia has fishing which will dwarf all the rest known in the world.' It was a prediction not quite to be realized, but the big-game fishing scene in Australasian waters is as spectacular as anywhere in the oceans.

Today, with our sophisticated hi-tech equipment, it is difficult to imagine how Grey coped during his titanic struggles with big fish; his rods were stiff, solid wood and his reels were huge centre-pins with a thumb-operated leather strip which acted as a brake when pressed against the spool.

He used a balloon to support a trolled bait near the surface (a method still used and thought to be 'new' not many years ago!) and was probably the first big-game angler to use a bamboo outrigger. We can only imagine what this brilliant angler would have achieved if he were equipped with today's advanced fishing gear.

But even before Zane Grey popularized deep-sea fishing, there were men who set out in small boats, their rods as thick and strong as medieval lances, with lines made of cuttyhunk (twisted linen), a name that lives on in the Cuttyhunk Fishing Club, founded in 1865, and based on an island of the same name in Massachusetts.

In those early times, there was little or no definition between the true deep-sea fishes and the large and powerful fish-like mammalian life of the sea: the porpoises, dolphins and small whale species.

For those early 19th-century pleasure anglers, with their flimsy boats, and the relatively low strength of the rods and lines at their disposal, there was always the threat of real danger if a big marlin, stronger than the fisherman himself, was hooked.

One of the really forward-thinking writers about all kinds of sea fishing was Frederick George Aflalo, a scientist and Fellow of the Zoological Society of London, who between 1891 and 1909 wrote learned books about all the known fishes and at the same time enjoyed fishing as a sport and pioneered big-game fishing as a special branch of sea angling.

In 1909 he published *Sunset Playgrounds* which described fishing in California, western Canada and the West Indies long before those prolific areas had been recognized for their big-game species.

Aflalo's *Sunshine and Sport in Florida and the West Indies* concentrated on tarpon fishing in those waters, while *Salt of My Life,* published in 1905, was one of the first volumes of sea-angling reminiscence.

Early fishing rods were made from bamboo and heavy greenheart wood, with wooden centre-pin reels. The lower model is a Starback.

An early spool of fishing line made by the well-known English tackle manufacturers Allcock & Co.

In this book Aflalo talked about fishing for what he called 'schnapper' (snapper) in Broken Bay in 1895 with members of the Kuriwa Schnapper Club. Most interesting was his opinion, after hand-lining for snapper of 2.2–2.7kg (5–6 lb), that rod and line would never cope with fish of double-figure weights. He was reeling-in one day when sharks moved in. By the time the terminal tackle reached the surface, the hooks held nothing but fish heads!

Ernest Hemingway is universally known for his novels *The Old Man and the Sea* and *Islands in the Stream*, but he also put his wonderfully descriptive prose to work in *Marlin off the Morro*. In his stories of fishing for striped and white marlin, the reader can practically smell the sea air and feel the spray. This book, published in 1933, should have a place on every sea angler's shelf.

Despite the creative efforts of these few sea angling writers, when compared with the number of books on freshwater game and coarse fishing, this branch of the sport has, until comparatively recently, been poorly served by literature. (The term 'coarse fishing' is very misleading and has nothing to do with its adherents, but serves to differentiate between fishing for members of the salmon and trout family and the other freshwater species such as pike, perch and numerous cyprinids). As historian Charles Chevenix Trench wrote in 1974 in the *History of Angling*: 'It is odd that sea fishing, which is probably the earliest form of angling, should have been, comparatively, so neglected.'

However, in the early years of the 20th century, some wealthy anglers began to roam the world in search of angling excitement. They were sportsmen such as Charles Frederick Holder, who described himself and his friends as 'men who like a dash of

F A Mitchell Hedges, author of Battles with a Giant Fish, *took this sawfish, measuring 9.4m (31ft), estimated at 2584 kg (5700 lb) off Panama in the early 1920s, after a fight lasting almost an entire day.*

The Bayano River, Panama, was home to F A Mitchell Hedges during the years he spent exploring the area.

spice with their pastimes'. With this in mind, Holder joined the Giant Ray Club, based at that time in Florida. Holder began with hand-lines, for this was the period when rod-and-line fishing for very large specimens was still only for the madman, as the reels and lines were not very strong.

As Holder put it: 'There is one stage in the playing of large fishes when the surest angler, while putting on a bold front, feels himself giving way before a relentless foe, supposed to be a victim to his skill. As I recall the really large fishes which I have taken with rod and reel, harpoon or cast line, I am inclined to confess the truth that I was often the one actually caught, and that the game was but adding to the under-the-sea gayety [sic] of the nations by playing me!'

An interesting comparison can be made when weights for rod-caught record fish are studied. In Holder's day the best albacore was a fish of 17.4kg (38 lb 11oz), taken by Gustave Frickman of New York; in 1998 the albacore all-tackle record stood at 40kg (88 lb 2oz) from Gran Canaria.

Another deep-sea angler of the early part of the century was F A Mitchell Hedges, a very different man from the rather gypsy-like Holder. Hedges was far-sighted for his time too; he despaired of big-game hunting with rifles, for it was 'conducive to indiscriminate slaughter and the sport has become confined to those who are fortunate enough to have a well-lined purse'. He preferred big-game fishing, for 'the hunting of beasts in their marine home is still in its infancy. There is a thrill and danger attached to it which will be welcomed by all true sportsmen...'.

In the 1920s, in the Gulf of Panama, Mitchell Hedges had a premonition about catching 'an enormous fish'. Using sides of meat cut from a sand shark as bait, he had two lines out, and early in the day one line began to move away. Mitchell Hedges does not give details of the line, but when it had all run out, his yacht, still anchored, was pulled along in the direction of the island of Morro. When the fish surfaced, Mitchell Hedges saw that he had hooked a gigantic sawfish. The struggle went on all day, with Mitchell Hedges and his helper being thrown overboard at one stage, but by late afternoon Mitchell

Sixteen sand sharks and a tiger shark, all caught on hook and line.

Hedges had managed to tow the sawfish into a bay, wind a manila line round its tail and anchor it to a rock. Mitchell Hedges then shot the huge sawfish twice in the head. The next morning it was found to measure 9.4m (31ft) long and weigh approximately 2584kg (5700 lb).

In 1929, C Mitchell Henry and Lt-Col. R F Stapleton, fishing the North Sea from Scarborough, on Britain's Yorkshire coast, contacted some very heavy fish which broke away. A year later, after upping their gear, they caught a 226.8kg (500 lb) tunny, a species seldom now seen in these waters. Although improved skills and advanced equipment bring new records, it is often at the expense of the species themselves.

THE BEGINNINGS OF CONSERVATION

The question of conservation never arose for the early sport fishermen, who took out all species of fish (both salt- and freshwater) by any means available. An angler by the name of A J Lane kept an angling diary in 1843, and one of his entries concerns spearing hundreds of freshwater fish, the very thought of which would give today's conservation-conscious angler apoplexy!

The mid-1930s saw the very first glimmerings of conservation – or at least of consideration – for fish, an approach that had been conspicuous by its absence until Mitchell Hedges spoke out against allowing any fish to take the bait right down when there was no intention of retaining it, calling it 'unsporting'. ('Taking the bait right down' describes the situation where the fish has been allowed to swallow the bait, leading inevitably to death once the barbed hook is lodged in its stomach.)

A hundred years ago, marine biologists were quite sure that the stocks of fish species we regard as food were virtually limitless: man, they said, could not influence their numbers with his puny commercial trawler fleets.

Those experts could not know that not only would the fleets grow enormously in numbers but that through their ability to scour the seabed clean of every living thing, edible or not, then raise their bulging nets to the surface where factory ships waited to salt and pack the catches, stocks would inevitably suffer. Throwing back unwanted fish does not work, because the pressure difference from seabed to surface kills most species anyway, whether the trawlers keep them or not. The fish have no time for the gas- or swim-bladder to adjust and the stomach becomes everted.

At first, fishing from commercial boats was done with men dropping individual lines for mackerel. In 1855 the *purse seine* (seine-net) was invented: 396m (1300ft) of tarred twine netting weighted at the bottom edge by lead, with cork floats at the top, scooping up anything in its path. Then came tub trawling, where trawlers carried six 91m (300ft) trawl lines with 1800 hooks.

'Sword boats' – those specifically trying for swordfish – were commercial long-liners. Using a main line 64km (40 miles) long, they followed the swordfish along the Grand Banks off Newfoundland

This bluefin tuna (Thunnus maccoyi) *displays streamlined grace and elegance in its natural environment.*

A BRIEF HISTORY

in the summer and down to the Caribbean in the winter, taking up to 15 tons of swordfish, which sold for hundreds of thousands of dollars.

By the mid-1980s the US commercial swordfish fleet comprised some 700 boats trailing a total of 50 million hooks a year. Between 1987 and 1991, the North Atlantic swordfish catch dropped from 20 million kg (45 million lb) to 15 million kg (33 million lb); the average size fell from 74.8kg to 49.8kg (165 lb to 110 lb).

In 1990 the International Commission for the Conservation of Tuna recommended a quota of 3.1 million kg (6.9 million lb) for US licensed boats.

Another threat to the world's food-fish stocks has been the use of drift nets. These floating 'walls of death', up to 50km (30 miles) long, entrapped any fish in their path and, together with the long-liners, decimated not only the surface-feeding food-fish in

Pelagic fish taken by seine-net trawling are a valuable food resource for humans and also form part of the food chain of many predatory game-fish species.

Commercial seine-net fishing.

many areas, but also the sharks, tunas, swordfish and wreckfish that feed off those food-fish. Other marine life also suffered, as dolphins, porpoises and whales became enmeshed and died by drowning.

CONSERVATION TODAY

In March 1994, *The Times* of London quoted a figure of 83,000 blue shark killed by commercial fishing in a single season. The United Nations then agreed to limit the use of drift nets, and the countries causing the most damage to fish stocks – South Korea, Taiwan and Japan – reluctantly agreed to a long-term programme to phase out drift nets.

The European Community (EC) followed by announcing a new maximum length of 2.5km (1.5 miles) for drift nets, but this elicited howls of rage when commercial fleets found their profits dropping. However, by 1998 a total worldwide ban on drift nets was on the books.

In their place, a new method, called 'rod and pole', has come into operation. This involves a combination of water-jets (which produce vibrations in the water) and small bait-fish, to attract tuna to the hook without entrapping other, unwanted species.

Meanwhile, at Loughborough, an English university, a research programme, sponsored by the Ministry of Agriculture, Fisheries and Food, has

produced a device designed to protect porpoises. Discs installed on commercial fishing nets recognize the sounds emitted by these marine mammals and transmit a similar sound back to the porpoises. This has the effect of stopping them from approaching the nets, where they can become enmeshed.

Quotas are now in force to limit the huge catches of common skate that are commercially fished from the North Sea. The average weight of this once prolific species, *Raja batis*, has been declining and it is estimated that between 1981 and 1995 all the females were netted (the shoals always contain a preponderance of females). Once prevalent in this sea, the species is now virtually extinct. Similar damage to fish stocks is occurring in every ocean.

Throughout the world, governments spend vast amounts of time and money trying to find a way of conserving food-fish stocks while at the same time carefully avoiding upsetting vested interests in commercial fishing businesses, whose profits depend upon every trawler in their fleets catching ton upon ton of food-fish on each trip they make out to their traditional grounds. Legislation abounds, of course,

laws have been passed, important-sounding committees have sat and deliberated over the years, statutory threats and press releases are handed out, but it is obvious to all but the politicians that there is no answer to the problem of who is to police the high seas. Banning drift netting is good on paper but it needs to be policed thoroughly.

The commercial threat to big-game fish stocks is not one of the pleasure angler's doing, although over the years far too many big-game fish (and all other species of sea fish) have been hooked and killed unnecessarily. From the author's personal experience, the species that has suffered the most are the thousands of sharks – mostly small blues – hooked and dragged aboard charter boats to die. Many of these are immature sharks that should have been carefully unhooked and released. We are upsetting the balance of nature by indiscriminately killing sharks and this will doubtless have long-term implications for the species as a whole.

All pleasure fishermen are sportsmen whose enjoyment of their chosen pastime places them in the category of hunter – and they share, albeit some-

This 386kg (850 lb) blue fin tuna was trolled off Nova Scotia, Canada.

what one-sidedly, the sport with the living creatures they seek. And so it is with the fishermen who seek the often very large and powerful species of sea fish described as big-game fishes. Unlike nature's hunters, who use their natural and instinctive abilities to seek, chase and pull down their prey, the sport fisherman has the advantage of human brain power, conscious thought, the ability to make decisions, and the technological aids of fish detection and fishing gear to find the quarry – which has nothing but the instincts of chase or evasion to guide its actions. If the species the fisherman is seeking is a predatory fish, then its aggression in taking a proffered lure can prove its undoing.

There are those who insist that fishing is a cruel, blood-thirsty activity, to be despised as an example of man's primitive and ancient background. Big-game fishermen need to consistently strive to make sure that their sport is not tarnished by misguided accusations of cruelty. One way for them to combat these accusations is to avoid unnecessary injury to the fish they catch. Those to be retained as food or bait must be killed quickly and without hesitation. Sharp raps on the top of the skull are usually effective in killing smallish fish quickly. Another method of quickly dispatching a small fish is to grasp it in gloved hands and bend the head up and back smartly to break the spinal cord.

The barbs of a hook are often said to be cruel and in freshwater fishing the use of the barbless hook is being widely adopted, as the barb does not lodge in the fish's lips or mouth and therefore more skill is needed by the angler to bring the fish to the net, for if the line is allowed to become slack the hook slips free and the fish is lost.

FISHING FOR THE FUTURE

At least 70 percent of the world's fisheries are over-exploited. For more than 50 years the International Game Fish Association (IGFA) has been promoting conservation by encouraging anglers around the world to adopt the techniques of tag and release, or catch and release.

More than 93 percent of all billfish brought to boat in Australian waters are tagged and released. Similarly, anglers in New Zealand, South Africa, the Americas and elsewhere are actively involved in tag and release programmes.

Releasing all fish, other than trophy catches or those for personal consumption, ensures the survival of the species and is fast gaining a reputation as the only sensible way to fish. Released fish survive to be caught again; they grow and spawn, thereby increasing future populations. Fishing with the

*In many parts of the world, including South Africa and Australia, the great white shark (*Carcharodon carcharias*) is a protected species which can only be captured on a tag and release basis.*

intention of releasing a fish requires a commitment on the part of the angler, as the fish has to be played and handled in such a manner as to ensure that it can be returned to the water alive, as tag and release done incorrectly merely results in the death of the fish and defeats the entire object of the exercise.

Anglers who participate in tagging programmes must ensure that data is correctly recorded and submitted to the relevant authorities, so that accurate records can be maintained. Among the data scientists are able to obtain from the records of fish tagged and released, as well as tagged fish that are

The ultimate expression of conservation. Proponents of tag and release know that by sustaining life they are preserving valuable resources for future generations. Gentle handling is necessary at all times to minimize distress to captured game fish.

recaptured, is information on fish stocks, migratory patterns and rates of growth, all of which contribute towards the long-term management of the species.

Many angling clubs now encourage their members to adopt catch or tag and release techniques as their normal method of fishing. The survival of the fish is the critical factor and there are various steps the angler must take if he intends to release his catch, as fish become easily stressed by capture and handling. Bringing the fish to boat as quickly as possible is one of the key elements in survival, as is water temperature, with fish becoming exhausted more rapidly in warm water than in cold.

Tackle must be chosen to ensure that fighting time is kept to a minimum: single hooks are easier to remove than double hooks; bait hooks, which are swallowed, cause greater injury than lures, which stay in the mouth; light tackle prolongs the fight and increases the risk of death.

Knowing how and where to place the tag is also important. Tags are normally placed near the base of the dorsal fin, above the lateral line, to avoid possible damage to the internal organs. Ideally, the tag should be placed while the fish remains in the water, but if this is not possible, then extreme care must be taken not to injure the fish or damage the skin as it is lifted on board and then lowered back into the water after tagging.

Before placing the tag, get the fish under control as much as possible. This requires co-operation amongst the crew and skipper, with all participants knowing the role they have to play so that handling and time out of the water are kept to a minimum. Once the tag has been placed, the hook must be removed if possible, or the leader wire cut down.

An exhausted fish must be allowed to recover before being released. With billfish, the most common method is to hold the fish by the bill and push the entire head under the water, while the skipper gently increases boat speed. The water flowing through the mouth and gills will revive the fish. The same result can also be achieved by moving the fish backwards and forwards through the water. As the fish revives, it will start to twitch and become active and, in the case of a billfish, will 'light up', that is, its natural iridescent colours will return. Now is the time to let go, knowing you have played a part in conserving the species for future generations.

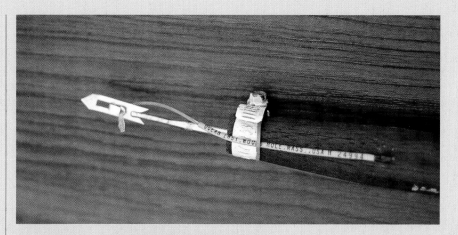

Above *A tag loaded and ready for use.*
Left *This longfin tuna (Thunnus alalunga),* or albacore, *has been tagged and is ready for release.*

The leader wire is cut down as short as possible.

The entire exercise should be swift and gentle, so that the fish recovers rapidly once it is returned to the water.

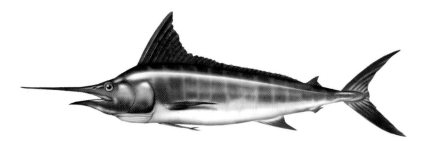

CHAPTER TWO

BIG-GAME SPECIES

Everyone knows that a fish has a backbone, fins, a tail and gills, and that it swims in water. But it is obvious that everyday language and simple descriptions are not accurate enough for proper scientific identification. So, a fish is a small-brained, cold-blooded creature with a skeleton of either cartilage or bone, and it breathes through gills that extract oxygen from the water in which it lives. Fish have existed since the dawn of time, but the details of how they evolved into today's huge number of species are not fully understood.

The reasons for this are probably that the first, primitive fishes arose in the Devonian period (350 million years ago) both in salt and fresh water, but when animals die in fresh water, this medium does not usually allow for creatures to become fossilized. In fresh water, predatory and bacterial action on a dead creature disperses its body parts, unlike in salt water, where the conditions at the bottom of deep seas are often anoxic (lacking oxygen), so bacterial decomposition does not occur, and fossilized skeletons remain more or less complete (articulated) when the sediment in which they are entombed turns to rock under the pressure of further sediments accumulating above.

Some of the oldest fish fossils are found in 350 million-year-old Devonian rocks, which formed in marine conditions. Many of these fish had armour-plated bodies and, in place of a mouth, an orifice into which food was taken. These ancient fishes are called agnathans (meaning 'without jaws').

Gnathic fishes (those with movable jaws) evolved towards the end of the Devonian period, the jaws developing from a pair of bony anterior (at/to the front) arches which support the gills. Some fossil

A black marlin (Makaira indica) *breaks the surface in an explosion of spray. To many anglers, capturing a fish like this represents the ultimate big-game challenge.*

fish are known by nothing more than hard spines and teeth, which give little evidence of the animal's shape, form or lifestyle. We do know, however, that as far back as the Devonian period fish had already begun evolving into the fully hard-boned species and the cartilaginous, shark-like fishes, which form the basis of the species we recognize today.

By the Carboniferous period (275 million years ago) the jawless fishes had become extinct and the soft-boned sharks, skates and rays (Class *Chondrichthyes*) and the bony fishes with true jaws (Class *Osteichthyes*) had taken their place. (Bony fishes did not evolve from the soft-boned species, they both evolved at the same time.)

The more structually advanced bony fishes (the *Teleosts*) developed into recognizable Classes by the Cenozoic period (65 million years ago) and within this group are placed all the present-day fish species, except the sharks, skates and rays.

There is an important reason for the Latin (and sometimes Greek) names which are often printed after the common names of all animals, although the angler may feel he has no reason to know these unless he has an intellectual interest in fish as a subject as well as a sporting interest in catching them. (One reason why the angler might be concerned to know the scientific name of his catch is when it is claimed as a rod-caught record for its species, and the positive identification depends upon it being scientifically described.)

Those two Latin/Greek names (sometimes three in the case of subspecies) are essential for the simple reason that whether a scientist speaks English, Russian, German, Chinese or any other language he will still recognize, for instance, *Thunnus alalunga*, as the albacore even if elsewhere it may be known as longfin tuna. Another example is the king mackerel, *Scomberomorus cavalla*, which is known variously as giant mackerel, kingfish and cavalla. Latin and Greek names are always printed in italics with the first name allotting the fish to a genus and carrying a capital letter, and the second giving it a species.

The list of big-game fish is long: it includes the larger members of the mackerel family (the albacore and the various tunas, the king mackerel and the Spanish mackerel), the wahoo, the giant sea bass, the dozen or so amberjacks, tarpon, snook, roosterfish, the large rays and skates, and the sharks such as the blue, hammerhead, mako, blacktip reef, tiger, porbeagle, thresher, white and tope.

The term 'big-game' fish is an arbitrary one and depends very much on location. Water temperature and currents have much to do with the distribution of big-game fish and man's liking for erecting boundaries is not always reflected in nature.

In the temperate-to-cold British waters, big-game fishing is mostly confined to the porbeagle, thresher, blue and mako sharks and the halibut, but other species are seen sporadically.

The eastern Atlantic, with its subtropical waters off the Azores, Canaries, coasts of Portugal and Spain, holds blue and white marlin, yellowfin tuna, spearfish, tarpon and of course blue, mako, porbeagle and smaller sharks. The western Atlantic has the same species, as well as barracuda, roosterfish and swordfish.

The eastern Pacific has most of the recognized big-game species, with the addition of dolphinfish, cobia and large non-big-game species.

The Mediterranean's subtropical waters hold swordfish, bluefin and yellowfin tuna, white marlin, and spearfish. Almost every big-game species is represented in Australasia and the Indian Ocean.

Some authorities feel that any species that consistently offers fish which top the 45.3kg (100 lb) mark, including the large skates and rays, should qualify for the title big-game fish.

The fish species listed below are those most often called 'big-game' fish. There is no definitive list, for it is largely parochial, and an Australian list, for example, would include species not seen in the Bahamas or the temperate areas of the eastern Atlantic. The International Game Fish Association (IGFA) is the universally recognized body whose world record rod-caught lists are universally accepted. Many other national federations issue their own lists, but most are affiliated to the IGFA and recognize its record-claiming procedures.

MACKERELS AND TUNAS

The Scombridae are a large group of pelagic oily fishes found in the tropical and subtropical seas of the world. They are powerful, torpedo-shaped fishes with pointed snouts and tapered tails. They vary greatly in size, from the huge bluefin tuna weighing nearly 680kg (1500 lb) to the smaller mackerels of 1.3kg (3 lb). Most are fierce predators and hunters.

King Mackerel

The king mackerel (*Scomberomorus cavalla*) is also known as the kingfish, couta, tanguigue, katonkel,

narrow-banded king, cuda and giant mackerel. It is a migratory species confined to the western coasts of the Atlantic Ocean from Cape Cod down to Brazil and is plentiful in the Caribbean at depths of between 10 and 20 fathoms. When compared with some big-game fish, this is not one of the bigger species, although it is the largest of the western Atlantic mackerels.

An identification point for this fish is the distinctive dip in the lateral line midway along the body. The rod and line record of 40.82kg (90 lb) comes from Key West, Florida, but commercially caught king mackerel can reach 45.3kg (100 lb).

Baits and fishing methods

Surface- or deep-trolled fish strips, small whole fish (mullet, herring, pinfish), live shrimp and trolled spoons can all be employed, as can drift-fishing with light-coloured jigs, feathers or plugs. Groundbaiting (chumming) is popular as an attractor.

Wahoo

Another member of the Scombridae family is the wahoo (*Acanthocybium solandri*), reputed to be the fastest fish in the sea, capable of bursts of 80kph (50mph), thanks to its slender, elongated body. Known as the peto, oahu fish and Pacific kingfish

depending on where it is caught, the wahoo is widespread in tropical seas including the Atlantic coast of the USA from Florida northwards, the Gulf of Mexico, Panama, Australia and South Africa.

It is one of the more colourful big-game fish with tiger-like blue stripes down the flanks (these disappear immediately after death). It has very strong teeth and, fairly unusually, the upper jaw is not fixed as it is in most fish, an odd feature that is an asset to this predator when it is attacking the prey fishes and squid on which it feeds. When the wahoo is investigated for scientific purposes, it is usually found to be host to large parasites in the stomach.

There is a record weight of 71.89kg (158 lb 8oz) from Loreto in Baja California, Mexico.

Baits and fishing methods

All kinds of bait attract the wahoo, including trolled mullet, Spanish mackerel, fish strips, squid and lures. If you are live-baiting for other species while the wahoo is in the vicinity, whatever method and bait you are using will very probably tempt it. A wire leader is a must if you expect this fish to be in the area, as its powerful teeth can bite through stout nylon.

The colourful, fast-moving wahoo will eagerly take a variety of bait and lures.

TUNAS Big-game anglers agree that, as a group, tunas provide the best sportfishing experience. They are amongst the fastest fish in the sea, with streamlined torpedo-shaped bodies and acute eyesight. The temperature of their blood does not reflect that of the surrounding water the way that of cold-blooded marine creatures does, but is raised when necessary by some muscular action. This explains why tunas are able to show so much stamina and reach speeds of up to 19kph (43mph) when hooked. All members of the *Scombridae* family, but particularly tunas, undertake wide-ranging migrations.

Albacore

For the angler, the albacore (*Thunnus alalunga*), known also as the longfin tuna, was once thought to exist as two species, one in the Atlantic, the other in the Pacific. However, taxonomists now consider them to be one species. One of the most widespread tunas it ranges through the warm and tropical seas, and while it is popular among big-game fishermen, it is also keenly sought by commercial interests because of its habit of migrating in large shoals (about 10 percent of the world tuna catch is albacore).

The albacore can be distinguished by its longer pectoral fins, the white line on the trailing edge of the tailfin and lack of spots on the body.

This fish can weigh over 36.3kg (80 lb), with the world record at 40kg (88 lb 2oz) taken off the Canary Islands. Commercially it has been caught accidentally to 45.3kg (100 lb).

Baits and fishing methods

Live or dead mullet, sauries, squid, herrings, anchovies, pilchards and other small fish drifted in a chum slick; trolled feathers, jigs and spoons; fly tackle, light tackle, depending on the feeding habits of the fish in the area you are fishing.

Big-eye tuna

The big-eye tuna (*Thunnus obesus*), a member of the Scombridae family, is widely distributed in deep oceans and easily mistaken for *Thunnus albacares*, the yellowfin tuna. A distinguishing characteristic is the striations which occur on the lower part of the liver. The big-eye is commercially exploited, mostly on longlines, but it is also a big-game fish, with the rod and line record weighing in at 197.3kg (435 lb) from Caba Blanca, Peru. The largest big-eye caught in the Atlantic weighed 170.3kg (375 lb), from Ocean City, Maryland.

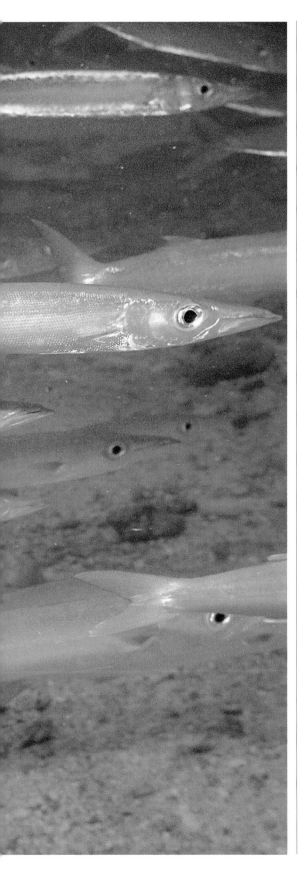

Baits and fishing methods

The big-eye feeds on mackerel, squid and krill, so follow the advice of 'big baits for big fish'. It takes its food anywhere from the surface down to the seabed, so deep-trolling with sizable fish (live or dead), whole squid, or lures is the way to catch big-eye.

Bluefin tuna

The bluefin (*Thunnus thynnus*) is the largest member of the tuna family, and one of the biggest bony fish, reaching weights of up to 907kg (2000 lb). The bluefin tuna's short pectoral fins distinguish it from its close relatives.

Highly migratory, the bluefin tuna's range extends throughout the Atlantic from the USA to the Mediterranean and the Black Sea, with suggestions that they reach as far north as Norway and Siberia, provided the water temperature remains above 10°C (50°F). In the southern hemisphere they are found in Australian and South African waters, where they are known by the common name, tunny.

The species first became known in the North Sea before World War II when a bluefin tuna weighing 386kg (851 lb) was caught.

In recent years commercial fishing, particularly by Japanese fleets, has made serious inroads into bluefin populations worldwide and consequently recreational angling for them has dwindled as the numbers have fallen. The world record is 679kg (1496 lb), from Aulds Cove, Nova Scotia, Canada.

Baits and fishing methods

When bluefin are spotted, use chum and large chunks of live or dead bait, or trolled squid and mackerel. Slow-trolling using pieces of hook bait as chum (known as 'chunking') works; sometimes the big ones will fall to artificial plastic lures or fish, spoons, feathers or squid. School bluefins may fall to fast-trolling using feathers or jigs.

The fast-swimming, aggressive great barracuda is widespread around the reefs and flats in most tropical seas. Schools normally comprise younger fish as the larger ones are usually loners.

33

Yellowfin tuna

The handsome yellowfin (*Thunnus albacares*) is very widespread and roams the tropical and sub-tropical seas of the world. As is the case with a few other tunas, yellowfin taken in the Pacific and

Atlantic oceans were originally thought to be different species, but they are in fact the same.

Like the other members of the species, yellowfin are migratory, following warm-water currents in search of food. They can reach weights of 200kg (440 lb). Although they can be confused with the big-eye and blackfin tunas, distinguishing features are the rows of whitish spots on the underside.

The name 'yellowfin' comes from Japanese fishermen who knew of it long before Charles Frederick Holder first encountered it in 1904, when he called it the 'Japanese tuna'. This is another tuna that is seriously threatened by commercial fishing, with a reported 1.5 million tons netted or taken on longlines annually, and populations are shrinking throughout the oceans.

A record weight of 176.3kg (388 lb 12oz) was recorded off San Benedicto, one of the Revillagigedo Islands, Mexico.

Baits and fishing methods

This tuna has a voracious appetite and a catholic taste in food, from smaller members of its own species to anchovy, shrimp and squid, krill and crustacean larvae, making the choice of bait difficult. Yellowfin are taken mostly during fast-trolling using cube bait or live fish. If coaxing is needed, groundbaiting (chumming) helps, as does skittering a live bait over the surface.

Blackfin tuna

The blackfin tuna (*Thunnus atlanticus*) occurs in the tropical and warm-temperate waters of the western Atlantic, where it is also known as the Bermuda tuna

or black-finned albacore. Its common name stems from the finlets which, unlike other tunas, have no yellowish tinge, remaining quite dark.

While not among the giants of the group, it can attain a weight of 22.6kg (50 lb). A fish of this size was recorded off Bermuda some years ago, although the present all-tackle record is 20.6kg (45 lb 8oz).

An interesting point about this tuna is that it is one of the favourite 'snacks' of the blue marlin.

Baits and fishing methods

Due to its size, this is another tuna partial to live pilchards and most smallish fish and squid. Fish strip or whole specimens of any local food-fish can be worked in a chum slick. Light tackle of all types can be successful. The skipper will suggest what to try on the day to obtain the most sport from the blackfin.

Dogtooth tuna

Found in the tropical waters of all the oceans, the dogtooth tuna (*Gymnosarda unicolor*), also known as the scaleless tuna, lizard-mouth or plain bonito, is

the pride of the Seychelles. It is also found in the Indian Ocean around the Comores islands and off Tanzania, as well as in the Red Sea. Another popular haunt is the Great Barrier Reef off the east coast of Australia.

The Atlantic dogtooth was once supposed to be a different species, but there is only one dogtooth tuna. The dogtooth's scales are so small that the fish appears scaleless, but this is not so.

The record weight of the dogtooth is 131kg (288 lb 12oz), from Kwan-Tall Island, Korea.

Baits and fishing methods

Skippers in the Seychelles have all the lures and jigs, but trolled fish, live or dead, is the best bet. The dogtooth finds much of its food in the small fishes that hover about reefs, so drift-fishing over reefs is another method, but this does not stop it taking any suitably-sized oily fish that might be offered.

Skipjack tuna

The skipjack (*Katsuwonus pelamis*) has a number of common local names including ocean skipjack,

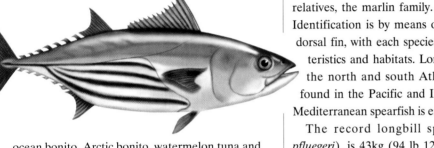

ocean bonito, Arctic bonito, watermelon tuna and striped tuna. Found in all tropical and subtropical seas, the skipjack is migratory, travels in large shoals and remains in blue water (the open sea).

A distinguishing feature is the series of longitudinal black stripes along the flanks. Not one of the larger tunas, the current record is 19kg (41 lb 14oz), caught off Pearl Beach, Mauritius.

The skipjack is an important food resource in Japan and India, where it is sold fresh or dried.

Baits and fishing methods

This tuna species has an exotic taste in food, taking lanternfish, surface-feeding prey species of most kinds, squid, shrimp and crustaceans. It will take a trolled whole but smallish fish, plugs and spoons and all kinds of trolled fish-baits. Jigging has also been known to attract the skipjack.

BILLFISHES

A number of groups of species of big-game fish are gathered under the embracing title of billfishes (the Istiophoridae). These groups are characterized by a pointed snout, an elongated extension of the upper jaw; and they include the spearfish and sailfish, which belong to the considerable and important group of marlins and swordfish. These fighting skills of these tremendously exciting "knights of the seas" provide some of the most gut-wrenching struggles to

be found in deep-sea angling. The interlocking nature of the vertebrae, which support the body muscles, enable the billfishes' great strength to be converted into speed and agility.

Spearfish

The three main members of this widespread group, the shortbill, longbill and the Mediterranean spearfish, are comparatively smaller than their mightier relatives, the marlin family. Identification is by means of the bill and high dorsal fin, with each species having its own characteristics and habitats. Longbill spearfish occur in the north and south Atlantic and shortbill are found in the Pacific and Indian oceans, while the Mediterranean spearfish is endemic to that area.

The record longbill spearfish (*Tetrapturus pfluegeri*), is 43kg (94 lb 12oz), from Puerto Rico, although a fish 1.8kg (4 lb) heavier was taken off Gran Canaria in 1980. Its shortbill cousin (*T. angustirostris*) is known to weigh 30kg (66 lb 2oz), a record from Narooma, Australia. The IGFA rod-caught record weight for the Mediterranean spearfish (*T. belone)* is listed as 41.20kg (90 lb 13oz), from Madeira.

Baits and fishing methods

These off-shore deep-water fish are fast, predatory surface feeders, taking any small or medium sized fish, including dolphinfish, sauries, flying fish, needle fish and squid. Light tackle is preferable for these fish.

Sailfish

True to its name, the sailfish has one outstanding physical attribute – the enormous dorsal fin which stands higher from the back of the fish than the depth of the body. It was long suspected that there were two species, *Istiophorus albicans* in the Atlantic, with a record weight of 64kg (141 lb) from Luanda, Angola, and *I. greyi*, 100.24kg (221 lb) from Santa Cruz, Ecuador. They have now been recognized as one and the same species and renamed *I. platypterus*.

This taxonomic quibble is of little concern to the angler, for wherever this fish is hooked, the aerial gyrations of the sailfish as it leaps from the surface, head shaking, creating small rainbows in the resulting spray before it plunges back beneath the waves, are exhilarating. The sailfishes are among the great sporting fishes. Putting back small ones is a sensible conservation move, and research suggests that they recover well when returned to the water.

Baits and fishing methods

Squid and octopus as well as many food-fish are taken. Oily fish-baits are recommended too, a safe bet with any predatory species. Trolled strip baits, whole ballyhoo, needlefish, flying fish, jacks, feathers and spoons are all effective. The mid-air acrobatics of these fish make for great excitement but their stamina is short lived, so light tackle is adequate and trolling probably the best method.

Broadbill swordfish

The most romantic of those difficult-looking Latin descriptions belongs to the broadbill swordfish (*Xiphias gladius*), so called due to the fact that its long sword is flattened, not round as is the case with the marlins and spearfish. The translation of its

Latin name is 'fish shaped like a sword'. The formidable 'sword' projecting from the head may have developed as a kind of frontal streamlining, but it is also used for striking at food-fish, stunning them before they are swallowed.

Broadbill are usually deep-water fish, occuring in tropical to temperate waters around the world. They often inhabit canyons and the deep-water banks at the edge of the continental drop-off. Night fishing, using lights to attract the fish, has become an increasingly popular way to catch broadbill.

The broadbill has been described as one of the toughest fish and a formidable prey. Swordfish have been known to attack boats, piercing up to 35.5cm (14in) of wood and embedding the sword so deeply that it has snapped off as the fish veered away, leaving the souvenir behind. The flesh of this fish is one of the great marine culinary delights of all time.

Broadbill swordfish can withstand the huge pressures that exist in deep water and have been seen at depths of 274.3m (900ft) and more by observers in a bathyscope. This popular, but elusive, big-game fish can reach weights of 453.6kg (1000 lb – the magical 'grander' mark). The record specimen of 536.1kg (1182 lb) was taken off Iquique, Chile.

Baits and fishing methods

The broadbill takes as its natural food practically any smaller fish, including squid, oily species such as mackerel, mullet, bonito, bluefish and any sizeable food-fish. It can sometimes be seen with its tall dorsal fin sticking up out of the water. Approach this fish with care, as it spooks easily. Tempt it at night by drifting a bait deep, or with quietly trolled squid.

MARLIN   Pre-eminent among the group collectively known as billfish are the marlins, tropical, warm-water species of the highest sporting calibre. There are differing opinions on specific names, and ichthyologists divide them into two main species, the black (or white, sometimes silver) marlin (*Makaira indica*), and the blue marlin (*M. nigricans*). However, the authoritative IGFA insists there are four species of marlin, the two already named, plus the striped (*Tetrapturus audax*), and the white (*T. albidus*). (Incidentally, 'white' describes not the external colour of this marlin, but that of the fish's flesh.) Important though such quibbling may be for taxonomists, it will never put a stop to anglers fishing for both (or all four!) in order to enjoy the thrills of marlin fishing.

To complicate matters further, the *Australian Zoologist* of 1954 listed two marlin in their waters which do not appear in Western taxonomic circles: Howard's marlin (*Istiompax mazara howardi*), and d'Ombrain's marlin (*I. d'ombrain*). It is probable that they are not specifically different but local variants of the blue marlin; when claiming records, the American Game Fishing Association (AGFA) insists on them both being shown as blue marlin.

Both variants are recorded as smaller than their relatives, with Howard's marlin reaching 219.5kg (484 lb) and d'Ombrain's marlin 80.7kg (178 lb). Incidentally, and as with many other fish species, the largest marlins caught are likely to be females, which reach heavier weights than the males.

Black marlin

The black marlin (*Makaira indica*) is highly sought-after by big-game anglers. It has been said of this species that it has 'the power, size and persistence of which anglers dream,' which adds up to a lot of pressure on black marlin throughout the world. It is hunted by Japanese and Russian commercial fishing interests, with a reported annual commercial catch totalling one million tons.

Confined mainly to the warm tropical areas of the Pacific and Indian oceans, migratory black marlin are occasionally taken on a long-line in the temperate Atlantic waters off Cape Town, South Africa.

The black marlin is unique in that it has pectoral fins which stand rigidly at right angles to its body and cannot be folded back. Its typically-shaped long dorsal fin does not stand as high as that of the blue, striped and white marlins.

A black marlin weighing 707.6kg (1560 lb) was caught off the coast of Cabo Blanco, Peru, but commercial fleets have seen them up to 907kg (2000 lb).

Baits and fishing methods

Trolled whole live fish, mackerel, dolphinfish, squid, bonito, flying fish and fish strip, as well as artificial lures, are all likely black marlin baits. A popular Australian end-tackle system is the use of three or four plastic squid with 16/0 hooks, known as the 'daisy rig', fished on a trace which is trolled off a reef. Whatever tackle you select, your rod, reel, line and terminal tackle have all got to be up to a fight if you intend to bring this giant of the sea to the boat.

A tagged black marlin is gently held by the bill until it has revived sufficiently to be released.

Blue marlin

The blue marlin (*Makaira nigricans*) is an ocean wanderer, swimming alone throughout the Atlantic, Pacific and Indian oceans, ranging the surface while feeding on shoal fish and squid. The pectoral fins of the blue marlin fold freely to the flanks, even after death, unlike those of the black marlin, which remain rigid. Perhaps because of the temperature difference between the Pacific and Atlantic and the consequent differing food-fish populations, the blue marlin of the Pacific seems to reach heavier average weights than its Atlantic counterparts.

The Atlantic record stands at 636kg (1402 lb) from Vitoria, Brazil, while the Pacific record is 624.1kg (1376 lb) from Kona, Hawaii.

Baits and fishing methods

Whole blackfin tuna, mullet, frigate and Spanish mackerel, bonito, whole dolphinfish, bonefish, flying fish; all local food fish; fish strip and squid; and artificial lures. Heavy line-class gear must be used for this species. Fast-trolling is the style.

White marlin

The white marlin is either *Tetrapturus albidus* or *Makaira albidus*, depending upon which authority one follows, but since this book is concerned with the sport of big-game fishing and its records, the first scientific description should be preferred because this is how the white marlin is shown in IGFA lists.

Confined to the Atlantic, this fish ranges the eastern seaboard of North and South America from Nova Scotia through the Caribbean and down to Brazil, although some reports suggest that it may move across the northern Atlantic as far as the Bay of Biscay, off the coast of Spain.

The white marlin has angled stripes down the flanks, like the blue and other marlins, but this fish is recognizable by the rounded edges of the dorsal fin and the tips of the pectoral and leading anal fins.

Not among the bigger marlins, its record stands at 82.5kg (181 lb 14oz), taken off Vitoria, Brazil.

Baits and fishing methods

Trolled small fish or fish strip, live ballyhoo, mullet, bonefish, mackerel, anchovy and herring. Since this predator takes any sizable fish it meets, a live one offered on the hook is favoured, but feathers and small spoons can be used, all on light tackle, as well as fast-trolled lures and artificials.

Striped marlin

The striped marlin (*Tetrapturus audax*) is also known as the stripey and, in Japan, the red marlin.

Confined to the Pacific and Indian Oceans, it can be identified by the more slender shape of the body, a factor which enables it to swim very fast, reaching speeds of up to 96kph (60mph) when chasing prey. When hooked however, this kind of speed is not met, for which anglers are grateful.

The striped marlin is famous for its acrobatic leaps from the sea while being played, and the glit-

tering spray thrown up during the fight is one of the abiding memories of a big-game fisherman. The jumps are thought to be instinctive movements based on the actions this fish has to take when going after fleeing food-fish skittering along the surface.

Its record weight stands at 224.1kg (494 lb), from Tutukaka, New Zealand.

Baits and fishing methods
Live fish, fish strip and lures. As another medium- or light-tackle marlin, the 'stripey' is usually fished for fairly close inshore where it feeds, so trolled whole local species are suitable baits, as are lures.

DOLPHINFISH

The dolphinfish (*Coryphaena hippurus*), a strange-looking, blunt-headed creature with a long dorsal fin and a strongly divided tailfin, has been described as resembling an 'exaggerated baseball bat'. This is particularly true in the case of the large males, with their high, vertical foreheads.

As the name has often caused confusion with the marine mammal more commonly known as a dolphin, the dolphinfish is now called the mahi mahi in most Pacific ports, and is also known in some parts of the world as the dorado.

One of the dolphinfish's distinguishing characteristics is its dramatic, iridescent blue-green and yellow colouring, although this fades quickly after death. A wide-ranging migratory fish found in temperate and tropical seas throughout the world, it is a deep water fish that remains on the surface in the midst of floating matter, including flotsam, which attracts smaller food fish. This highly-rated game fish makes exceptionally good eating.

One of the hot-spots for the dolphinfish is the Great Barrier Reef, where it reaches over 36.2kg (80 lb), although the heaviest rod-caught record is 39.4kg (87 lb) from Costa Rica.

Baits and fishing methods
These extremely fast swimmers will take live fish, flying fish, mullet, balao, squid, fish strip and artificial lures. Dolphinfish are taken by trolling with live bait or lures. When a shoal is sighted, chumming can bring them quite close and then lures or small pieces of fish often yield multiple catches. (It is believed

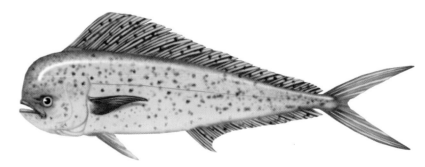

that if you take one dolphinfish, the rest of the shoal will stay to be caught as well). Use light gear to fish with whole or strip bait, trolled or suspended; artificials are also good.

A striped marlin is brought to the boat.

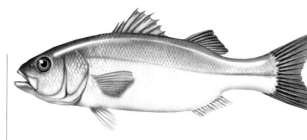

ROOSTERFISH

A strange name for a strange-looking fish! Also known as papagallo (Mexican for 'head rooster'), the roosterfish (*Nematistius pectoralis*), derives its name from the cockscomb appearance of the second dorsal fin, which has one spine and a number of soft rays. The 'rooster' effect becomes apparent when the fish is chasing prey or has been hooked.

The dorsal fins, which normally lie flat along the fish's back, become erect and the fish may leap repeatedly over the surface. The roosterfish has dark blue or black backward curving stripes on its flanks. An inshore fish, it inhabits the surf and sandy bottoms at moderate depths.

It is found in the eastern Pacific from California south down to Peru, with a concentration off the coast of Ecuador, while there have been sightings off the Galápagos Islands.

In most areas the roosterfish has a local commercial value as it is a tasty eating fish. A solitary species, it seems to have been ignored by some official fish listings although it has an official IGFA record weight of 51.7kg (114 lb), caught off La Paz, in Baja, Mexico.

Baits and fishing methods

The roosterfish feeds on small fish, so use small dead and live baits or lures. The greyhound-like activities of the roosterfish when hooked or in pursuit of prey makes it suitable for trolling in blue water or inshore with smallish whole fish or lures.

GIANT SEA BASS

The giant sea bass (*Stereolepis gigas*), also called the California black sea bass or California jewfish, occurs in tropical and subtropical waters off the coasts of California and Mexico. The largest specimens are reported to have a lifespan up to 75 years.

Anglers need not steam out into deep blue water to find the giant sea bass, as despite its great bulk, it is an inshore fish found rarely in waters deeper than 25 fathoms. A popular eating fish, commercial fishing has made inroads into the stocks of this species.

The rod-caught record for the giant sea bass is 255.6kg (563 lb 8oz) from Anacapa Island off California; other large specimens have been taken from this area.

Baits and fishing methods

Live or dead fish and large natural baits are best. The giant sea bass is a bottom-feeding fish, so your bait must be down there too. Use whole fish or any other animal food such as shellfish or crab.

JEWFISH

The jewfish (*Epinephelus itajara*) goes under several names, including spotted grouper and junefish. It is found on both sides of the North American coast, from Florida to Brazil on the west coast and from Costa Rica to Peru on the Pacific coast. It is one of three groupers, the others being the groper, or garrupa (*E. lanceolatus*) which is confined to seas off the East African coast, Australasia and the western Pacific; and the recently named vielle tukala (*E. tukala*) found in the western Indian Ocean. Extremely curious fish, there are wonderful reports of the jewfish 'inhaling' turtles into their cavernous mouths and even trying to swallow divers 'out of curiosity'!

In common with a few other species of grouper, it seems that all jewfish are born female, changing to males at a later stage in life when the population experiences an instinctive and collective need for some males to develop.

All three groupers are of impressive size, with the IGFA rod-caught record jewfish at 308.4kg (680 lb), from Fernandina Bank, Florida; the groper record an equally sizable 272kg (600 lb), from Australia; while the vielle tukala is reported to reach 'only' 108.8kg (240 lb).

Baits and fishing methods

Bottom-fished mullet, grunts, mackerel, crabs, spiny lobsters, conches, clams and fish heads. These are not very sporting fishes, often retreating into a hole or between rocks when hooked. Sink the bait (live or dead fish) to the bottom (which will be shallow in spite of the jewfish's size). It makes good eating, with fine, succulent white flesh.

BARRACUDA

There is no mistaking the long, lean, menacing shape of this fish with its mouthful of sharp teeth. The IGFA record list includes four barracuda: the blackfin, the great, the Mexican and the slender, but this differs from the scientific grouping, which identifies the great barracuda (*Sphyraena barracuda*), the California or Pacific barracuda (*S. argentea*), and the guaguanche (*S. guachancho*).

The barracuda is not related to the barracouta – gemfish, snoek or barracuta (*Rexea solandri*) – common in South African and southern Australian seas. It is found mostly in the western Atlantic and the Caribbean, but inhabits tropical seas everywhere, with the exception of the eastern Pacific.

A rapacious predator which feeds almost entirely on fish, barracuda can be found close inshore or out in blue water; and have been hooked both on the surface and at depths of 71m (200ft) and more.

The great barracuda is a known cause of ciguatera (a nerve poisoning) when eaten and anglers are advised to exercise caution. In terms of weight, which brings it into the big-game range of fishes, the great barracuda's current rod-caught record is 38.55kg (85 lb) from

the Philippines, although a previous record stood at 46.7kg (103 lb), so there is room for improvement. (Fishing records can be, and often are, amended, or even deleted, if information casting doubt on an accepted record comes to light.)

Baits and fishing methods

This fish is a prime predator, so the bait will be live small fishes, plugs, spoons, prepared baits or anything that will trigger off an attack. Fishing methods include freshwater techniques such as casting and retrieving using heavier salt-water gear, baits or lures. It is essential to keep the bait on the move.

A barracuda that has fallen prey to a lure shows the sharp predatory teeth that have earned it a reputation as a fierce fighter.

BLUEFISH

The bluefish (*Pomatomus saltatrix*) is also known as the tailor, elf, shad or chopper. The sole member of its genus, and somewhat pugnacious-looking, it lives up to yet another of its local appellations, the marine piranha, for it bites anything in sight when feeding, even following a prey-fish as it is lifted out of the water. Many unfortunate anglers have found themselves victims of the bluefish's sharp teeth. The bluefish has a world-wide distribution which includes the eastern coast of the USA, the Mediterranean and the Black Sea, as well as New Zealand, Australia and South Africa, which explains its many common names.

The streamlined bluefish gets its name from its coloration, an attractive blue-green becoming lighter toward the ventral area.

Many record specimens have been taken off the coast of North Carolina, with the rod-caught record being 14.4kg (31 lb 12oz).

Baits and fishing methods

Pilchards, anchovies, squid, lures, jigs, feathers and plugs are all used to catch bluefish. The methods of bait presentation can be trolling, jigging or casting when drifting. When a shoal is seen, do not assume that a lure drawn through them will result in a capture, it will only cause them to go into a swift dive.

COBIA

The fact that the cobia (*Rachycentron canadum*) has a worldwide distribution guarantees it a long list of local names – sergeantfish, lemonfish, black salmon, crab-eater, runner, prodigal son and black kingfish being a few. A predator, it is the only member of its family. Its menacing, lean shape gives it a superficial resemblance to remora and small sharks although its snout is turned slightly up and the mouth is not underslung. The cobia also has some affinity with sharks, for it accompanies groups of sharks in their ocean wanderings. The record comes from Shark Bay, Western Australia, a weight of 61.5kg (135 lb 9oz).

Baits and fishing methods

As a strong-fighting big-game fish, the cobia is best sought by trolling either with fishbait or lure, or heavy spinning tackle. It is also fished for from inshore marks, using hooked crab or shellfish.

YELLOWTAIL

A widespread, well-liked moderately sized fighting fish, the yellowtail kingfish (*Seriola lalandi*) is a member of the Carangidae family and bears a close resemblance to the greater amberjack, to which it is related. It is a coastal schooling fish and a fast swimmer. The colour of its caudal (tail) fin supplies the reason for its name and there is a spiny first dorsal fin. Found on both sides of the equator, three sub-species are recognized, the California, Asian and southern yellowtail, each of which appears to remain

isolated from the others, without any interaction. This is a hard-fighting predatory species with a record weight of 52kg (114 lb 10 oz) from Tauranga, New Zealand.

Baits and fishing methods

Yellowtail can be taken on trolled or cast oily live bait or on lures. They do well in blue water, but are often caught close in-shore by handline fishermen. On occasions, whole shoals may follow a hooked or struggling fish to the surface, providing waiting anglers with an easy catch. The yellowtail is generally regarded as a good eating fish.

GREATER AMBERJACK

The greater amberjack (*Seriola dumerili*) has an enormous range and can be found in the seas of the eastern and central Pacific, western Atlantic, off the west coast of Africa and in the Mediterranean; coupled with this range, the greater amberjack swims at any depth from the surface to the seabed.

The greater amberjack's reputation with the big-game angler stems from its willingness to strike at almost anything it is offered. When hooked it fights like a trojan. This is another fish that can pass on ciguatera poisoning.

There is a recorded weight of 80.2kg (177 lb) from Trinidad, but the IGFA record is 70.6kg (155 lb 10oz) from the Challenger Bank, Bermuda.

Baits and fishing methods

Live mullet, grunts, pinfish or other small fish, or fish strip. The greater amberjack takes all varieties of trolled baits and artificials, including lures, spoons and plugs, but a live food-fish on a hook also attracts this fish. Greater amberjack have been hooked at a depth of 250 fathoms.

BLACK DRUM

The black drum (*Pogonias cromis*) is a fish of the western Atlantic, from Massachusetts southwards past Florida and the Gulf of Mexico, down to Argentina. One of a number of drums, it is also known as the croaker. The name 'drum' comes from the male fish's specialized muscle that vibrates against the swim-bladder and causes a very audible sound, presumably made to attract females.

For a fish that dwells inshore, the black drum has a huge record weight of 51.3kg (113 lb 1oz), from Delaware, USA, although this must have been a rare specimen, most being only half that size.

Baits and fishing methods

Bonefish, shrimp, clam, squid or crab; metal diamond jigs, spoons, and a fly called a bucktail, which imitates a small fish. A bait of crab, shellfish, prawn,

squid, or drift-fishing with a lure fished on the bottom is the method usually employed, but the drum is not noted as being a doughty fighter.

TARPON

Here is yet another confusion between taxonomists. The IGFA recognizes one species, but other authorities suggest there are two; one in the Atlantic, *Tarpon atlanticus*, and the other in the Indo-Pacific, *Megalops cyprinoides*. Here, the single-species IGFA ruling is followed. It could be suggested that the tarpon should not be considered as a salt water game fish since many specimens are caught from brackish water, estuaries and mangrove swamps, even far as 161km (100 miles) inland, but it is primarily immature tarpon that are found in these places because of the cover they provide from the tarpon's predators.

Very large scales, a pugnacious-looking protruding lower jaw and a bright silver coloration are the prime features of this tropical and subtropical fish. Because it is considered virtually inedible by man the commercial fishing industry leaves it alone.

The magnificent tarpon is considered to be one of the really great sporting fishes, with dual record weights (because of its Atlantic and Indo-Pacific habitats) of 128.36kg (283 lb) from Lake Maracaibo, Venezuela; and, remarkably, very nearly the same weight from Sherbro Island, Sierra Leone, of 128.5kg (283 lb 4oz).

Baits and fishing methods

If you want to hook one and enjoy the fight with no hope of boating it, try fly-fishing for tarpon. Otherwise get out the 24kg (50 lb) gear with a strong wire leader, and use live fish or squid or troll with artificial lures.

GIANT TREVALLY

The giant (or great) trevally (*Caranx ignobilis*) is also known as the kingfish, giant kingfish, jack, karambisi, turrum and the ulus. The trevallies belong to the large and mixed Carangidae family, which comprises up to eight species.

They are plentiful in the Indian and Pacific oceans, around Australia and New Zealand, and are also found off Kenya in East Africa and around the islands of Hawaii.

The giant trevally grows to over 62kg (130 lb). The body and head are usually very deep, the snout blunt, and the lateral line curves towards the tail.

The rod-caught record stands at 65.9kg (145 lb 8oz), from Makena, Maui, Hawaii.

Baits and fishing methods

The giant trevally is a large, aggressive predator and an exceptionally strong game fish that fights to the end. Dusk and dawn are when the angler should be out trying for this powerful fighter, which is best caught using live bait.

HALIBUT

These very heavy flatfishes occur throughout the Atlantic and the Pacific. The Atlantic halibut (*Hippoglossus hippoglossus*), known as the common halibut, giant halibut and right-eye flounder, is found in the deep, cold waters of the North Atlantic from the New Jersey coast up to Iceland and across to Britain.

The Pacific halibut (*H. stenolepis*), also called the northern halibut, right halibut and alabato, occupies the cold waters of the north Pacific from San Francisco up to Alaska and across to Japan.

One of the wonders of marine biology is the 'migratory eye' of these flatfishes. Born 'pelagic, bilaterally symmetrical and upright' (i.e. like an ordinary fish in appearance), the 2.5cm (1in) larvae turn on to one side after a few weeks, and one eye moves over the skull to come to rest near the other. They then spend the rest of their lives swimming 'eyeless side' down – which gives rise to the name 'flatfish'.

These flatfishes are among the biggest bony fishes in the world, and it requires all the angler's strength to reel them up from the deep waters they prefer – they are known as down as far as 800 fathoms.

The largest known specimen, taken off Sweden, tipped the scales at 326.6kg (720 lb). Current record weights are Atlantic halibut, 115.78kg (255 lb 4oz), from Massachusetts; and Pacific halibut 208.2kg (459 lb), from Dutch Harbour, Alaska.

Baits and fishing methods

A variety of fish and crustaceans found in mid-water and on the bottom are eaten, so baits will be the same. Try drift-fishing with whole or large fish strips, using strong tackle. Halibut have also been hooked on large diamond jigs.

SNOOK

The subtropical waters of central America and the Gulf of Mexico are the domain of the snook (*Centropomus undecimalis*), with six species occur-

ring on the Atlantic coast and a further six in the Pacific. Warm water is essential for this species' survival and they inhabit shallow coastal waters, estuaries and lagoons, where they are caught on rod or by fly casting. They are distinguished by their protruding lower jaw and prominent black lateral line.

Snook make excellent eating and are part of a family that includes the giant Nile perch (*Lates niloticus*) and the barramundi (*Lates calcarifer*). The common snook must not be confused with the snoek (*Thyrsites atun*) which is not a big-game fish.

The record line-caught snook, 26.19kg (57 lb 12oz), was taken off Costa Rica.

Baits and fishing methods

The best time for fishing is on the changing tide. Try trolling or casting artificial lures; or use live bait, including shrimps, crabs and small fish.

CARTILAGINOUS FISHES

In contrast to the bony fishes described earlier, one of the features that distinguishes this group, which includes sharks, rays, guitarfishes and sawfish, is the structure of the skeleton, which is composed of cartilage, not bony tissue.

SKATES AND RAYS

Many ray and skate species are found throughout the world, but few attain the sort of weight which might admit them to the league of big-game fishes. There are exceptions: the butterfly ray (*Gymnura natalensis*) reaches 60kg (132 lb 4oz); and the common skate (*Raja batis*), over 63.5kg (140 lb).

The latter has a Scottish and IGFA record of 97kg (214 lb) and an English record of 102.9kg (227 lb). An Irish rod-caught record of 100.2kg (221 lb) was either not submitted to the IGFA for world ratification, or for some reason turned down. The variation in these records reflects differences in possible weights in areas covered by the authorities.

A more exotic fish, the manta, batfish, or giant devil ray (*Manta* sp.), which underwater film-makers love to record 'flying' gracefully through the water, is not fished for – which is just as well because it reaches weights of 360.7kg (3000 lb)!

Baits and fishing methods

Fishing for the common skate is carried out on the seabed with heavy tackle and whole mackerel or large strips as bait. Skates and rays are bottom-feeding fishes and they take a bait by settling down on it and engulfing it in their huge underslung jaws.

When the strike occurs, skates and rays use their wings like a suction pad to hold tight to the seabed, so playing them can be an exhausting business.

SAWFISH

The sawfish (*Pristis* spp.) belongs to a group of soft-boned flatfishes. Their preferred habitat is shallow water, which is the reason why big-game anglers generally have little to do with them.

The 'saw' is an elongation of

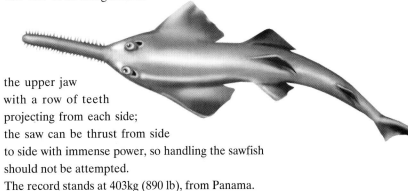

the upper jaw with a row of teeth projecting from each side; the saw can be thrust from side to side with immense power, so handling the sawfish should not be attempted.

The record stands at 403kg (890 lb), from Panama.

Baits and fishing methods

The sawfish is of no interest to deep-sea anglers but is accidentally hooked, hence the rod-caught record.

SHARKS

Among the distinguishing physical characteristics of the more than 350 species of shark found worldwide are the cartilaginous skeleton, the lack of scales, the jaw mechanism and the teeth. The latter are frequently used to provide species identification, but close inspection of their dentition can only be carried out after death.

The many sensational press reports of shark attacks on bathers in various parts of the world have given sharks an undeservedly bad reputation. However, these marine predators attack only when instinct triggers off either a feeding or a defensive mode. Unlike man, they do not 'decide' to attack purely from dislike. Sharks have an incredible ability to detect blood in the sea at a concentration as low as one millionth part blood to water, and then to home in on the source (this ability also allows them to home in on your freshly caught bait-fish). Since it was discovered that some shark meat is not only edible but tasty, certain

species have dwindled in numbers. Catching sharks of any kind was once thought very macho, but this is no longer the norm and a number of species are now protected in different parts of the world.

The Greenland shark (*Somniosus microcephalus*), also known as the gurry shark, has a listed IGFA rod-caught record of 775kg (1708 lb 9oz), off Trondheim, Norway. Since its habitat is the North Atlantic, from Maine past the Arctic Circle and eastwards to Britain and across the North Sea, little has been written about it with angling in mind – big-game anglers generally prefer tropical and subtropical waters and the accompanying sunshine. The Greenland shark has a catholic appetite, however, as evidenced by the fully grown caribou that was found in the stomach of one specimen.

Blue shark

It is probable that the shark that has suffered most from unnecessary killing is the blue shark (*Prionace glauca*), a well-shaped fish with long pectoral fins. It is also known as the blue whaler, or whale shark (because of its habit of once following whaling ships in the days when unwanted carcasses were discarded by simply being dumped overboard). The blue shark is found all over the world in tropical and subtropical seas; as well as in northern areas, such as the British Isles, on occasions when the water becomes warmed by long hot periods.

Juvenile blues, many only 0.9 – 1.5m (3 – 5ft) long, have been hauled by the thousand into boats by anglers who have then boasted about their angling prowess, even though the blue is well down in the shark fighting list.

It seems, thankfully, that some sense has taken over and that anglers everywhere are releasing anything under 45.3kg (100 lb), although even that is rather low for the survival of some species.

The blue shark is the most common shark species worldwide, with a record weight of 205.9kg (454 lb), from Martha's Vineyard, Massachusetts.

This is probably as close as most anglers want to get to a blue shark.

Baits and fishing methods

Not one of the largest sharks, the blue can be fought on an under-44kg-class (20 lb) rod and the angler should allow fresh mackerel – the best bait, but other oily species will do – whole, in strips or in a cocktail, to settle in the trail of chum. Since sharks home in on their food by smell, using their ultrasensitive nasal organs, groundbaiting (chumming) is the traditional way of bringing them to the hook-bait.

Hammerhead shark

There should be no problem in identifying this shark's flattened, hammer-shaped head with the eyes situated at each end of the protuberances. There are three species: the great hammerhead (*Sphyrna mokarran*), the bonnethead or shovelhead shark (*S. tiburo*), which has two subspecies, and the smooth hammerhead shark (*S. zygaena*). All three are normally found in tropical and subtropical waters, but they have also been seen in the Mediterranean and English Channel during warm spells.

In common with all the sharks, smell – not sight – seems to be the main sense employed in finding food. As it approaches its prey fish, the hammerhead swivels its head from side to side, using each eye in turn, as the optic nerves cannot produce a combined image. Although not among the largest sharks, the record great hammerhead of 449.5kg (991 lb) was caught off Sarasota, Florida.

The smooth hammerhead record is 148.10kg (326 lb 7oz), from Hawke's Bay, New Zealand.

Baits and fishing methods

All prey fish, dead or alive, can be used while trolling slowly, drifting, or even hanging the fish bait down where an echo-sounder has shown hammerheads to be feeding. Suspended baits work well, with the line supported at the desired depth by a balloon.

Mako shark

An ocean-going shark, the shortfin mako (*Isurus oxyrinchus*) was once thought to be present in the Atlantic, Indian and Pacific oceans, but the Pacific species has been named the bonito shark (*I. paucus*). As with many fish species round the world, the mako has a number of local names, including shortfin mako and sharp-nosed mackerel shark. 'Mako' is a Maori term and this fish has been represented in their rock carvings, with the menfolk wearing the shark's teeth in their ears.

Described by Zane Grey as 'the most aristocratic' of all sharks, the mako shark has striking blue flanks, which fade to grey on death.

Makos may prey on small swordfish; there is a report of one weighing 331.1kg (730 lb) which, when killed and opened up, was found to have a complete 58.9kg (130 lb) swordfish in its stomach.

Many American anglers seem not to regard sharks as qualifying for the description 'big-game fish', but they make an exception in the case of the mako in view of its fighting qualities and speed.

The IGFA lists a record mako weighing 505.7kg (1115 lb), taken off Black River, Mauritius. The British record of 226.7kg (500 lb), was taken off the Eddystone Rocks, Cornwall.

Baits and fishing methods

Remember: 'big fish, big bait', and few sharks come bigger than a big mako. Lots of groundbait (chum) will raise interest, then trolled whole tuna and other oily fish (dead or alive) should do the trick; lures work, too, but fish meat is their food. Of course, anglers fishing for shark – or any other huge gamefish – will ensure that their tackle is more than up to the fish they are seeking.

Porbeagle shark

The porbeagle (*Lamna nasus*), also known as the mackerel shark or herring shark because of its diet, is common round the world as a blue water fish.

Although it usually keeps to temperate seas, the porbeagle shark has the ability to raise its body temperature, which explains its presence in the cold waters of the Gulf of St. Lawrence in Canada, off Iceland and Norway, and in the Mediterranean. It is often seen in the eastern Atlantic and the English Channel.

As it is not known to put up much of a fight, informed opinion does not include the porbeagle among the big-game sharks, but the IGFA lists it with a record of 230kg (507 lb) from the Pentland Firth, Caithness, Scotland.

Baits and fishing methods

The porbeagle is big and active, and the angler's gear must match it. Live mackerel makes a fine bait for all sharks because they are the ultimate predators, so if your moral attitude to live bait allows it, use it. Groundbait (chum) is the first thing to go overboard, followed, when the slick stretches out nicely, by trolled whole fish – the oilier the better.

Thresher shark

The obvious identification mark of the longtail thresher (*Alopias vulpinus*) is the extremely elongated upper lobe of the tailfin. When feeding, the thresher (also known as the fox shark, sea fox, swiveltail and swingletail), uses this lobe to 'herd' foodfish into packs, then employs it as a weapon to stun them.

The thresher shark is found worldwide. The record is 348kg (767 lb 3oz), taken off the Bay of Islands, New Zealand. The record Atlantic/Pacific bigeye thresher (*A. superciliosus*), weighing in at 363.8kg (802 lb), was also taken off New Zealand.

Baits and fishing methods

Use a 24kg class (50 lb) rod and one of the biggest big-game reels that will hold at least 365m (400yd) of 24kg (50 lb) line, because a big, hooked thresher will be off and away like a speedboat.

Marlin-trolling methods are ideal with foodfish bait, either deep or allowing the bait to drift. Marlin-type lures and other artificials can be tried. It has been known for thresher flesh to be used as a bait for other sharks.

Tiger shark

The powerful and dangerous tiger shark (*Galeocerdo cuvieri*), also called the leopard shark, gets its name from the brownish grey stripes that run down its upperside.

The tiger shark occurs worldwide in tropical and subtropical waters, and has been seen as far north as Iceland.

A fish with a vast, omnivorous appetite, the stomach contents of the tiger shark have been shown to include tar paper, shoes (without evidence of the owner!), tins of canned fish, bottles, coal and animal remains (dogs, cats and even crocodiles, as well as fish, other sharks, crustaceans, sea lions and turtles). Tiger sharks frequent shallow waters and have been known to attack bathers off American beaches and elsewhere. They are sluggish swimmers, only coming alive in the presence of food. However, they do not have the stamina of other sharks and, after a strong initial resistance, do not put up much of a fight.

The IGFA record is 807.4kg (1780 lb), caught off Cherry Grove, South Carolina, USA.

Baits and fishing methods

The tiger shark will eat practically anything it can swallow. Whole fish or unwanted meat (it isn't particular about condition) will interest this fish. Trolling or suspended baits are used after groundbaiting (chumming).

If tiger sharks are about while you are after other big-game species, you might find yourself reeling in both the sought-for fish and a tiger. Hang on and if you have heavy gear, you might get both!

Great White Shark

The great white shark (*Carcharodon carcharias*) is one of the largest and most powerful predators on earth. Also called the white pointer, blue pointer and white death, it is this fish that triggered off the Hollywood concept of malevolent, man-eating sharks, made famous in the movie *Jaws*.

The great white shark is naturally extremely aggressive, but its usual diet consists of marine mammals – mostly seals, bony fish and rays – rather than men and boats. The longest great white measured was 11.2m (37ft), while one taken off Cuba measured 6.4m (21ft) and weighed 3312kg (7302 lb) – no tiddler this!

Occurring in all the tropical and temperate seas, mostly in blue water along the continental shelf, the great white shark has been seen off northern Spain, in the Mediterranean and the Adriatic, while in the western Atlantic it has reached as far north as Nova Scotia. In the Pacific it roams all round Australia, where in the past spectacular catches were made by anglers such as Alfred Dean, who caught six great whites weighing over a ton.

Australian big-game fisherman and author Peter Goadby writes: 'The feature most remarked on by those who have seen great white sharks in action is the huge dark eye which forces itself into the human mind by its apparent intelligence, ferocity and constant watchfulness ... it seems to resemble a silent giant bomber.'

This is the shark which most often attacks boats, sometimes leaving teeth as a reminder of its power.

The record great white was a massive 1208.3kg (2664 lb) specimen caught in the late 1950s by Alfred Dean off Ceduna, South Australia. The species is now protected in many countries, including Australia, the USA and South Africa.

Baits and fishing methods

If you have released groundbait into the water, you could find a great white shark following the slick right up to the boat. However, if you plan to hook one, use trolled meat or large, whole oily fish. You'll need really heavy gear and nerves of steel!

The great white shark is one of the most powerful, and feared, predators on earth.

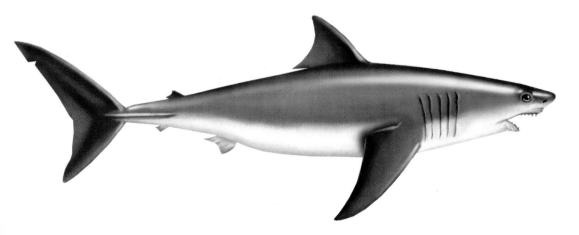

A whitetip shark cruising the depths. The identifying white fin tips are clearly visible.

Whitetip sharks

Scientists recognize three sharks in this genus: the reef whitetip (*Carcharhinus albimarginatus*), oceanic whitetip (*C. longimanus*) and the bull, or Zambezi, shark (*C. leucas*). They can be recognized, as implied by the name, by the characteristic white tips on the rear edges of all fins.

Whitetip sharks are widespread, occuring in tropical and subtropical waters throughout the world.

The bull shark is able to live in fresh water for long periods and frequently enters rivers and estuaries, often travelling many kilometres upstream. It is known to attack bathers in shallow water.

IGFA records list the oceanic whitetip at 66.4kg (146 lb 8oz), from Kona, Hawaii; the reef whitetip at 18.25kg (40 lb 4oz), from Isla Coiba, Panama; and the bull shark at 222.3kg (490 lb), from Dauphin Island, Alabama – all within the big-game league.

Baits and fishing methods

These are not particularly active sharks, and anglers are not likely to make serious efforts to fish for them. However, they have occasionally been caught by shore anglers using live bait, providing curiosity value for onlookers.

The rod-caught record is 30.8kg (67 lb 14oz), from Mcloughins Beach, Victoria, Australia.

A related fish, the smoothhound, or houndshark (*M. mustelus*), which has white spots on its dorsal area and along the lateral line, is fished for in the eastern Atlantic and English Channel, reaching weights of 28kg (17 lb 8oz).

Tope

In some parts of the world the tope is not thought of as a big-game fish, but one particular species *Galeorhinus australis* (also known as the school shark in Australia), has a recorded weight of 22.6kg (50 lb) and therefore would

appear to be a proper candidate.

Another tope, *G. galeus* (also called the toper or sweet william), is an eastern Atlantic and North Sea fish, with a rod-caught record of 37.4kg (82 lb 8oz), from Bradwell-on-Sea, Essex, England. The soupfin shark, *G. zyopterus,* (known as the oil shark or vitamin shark), is found in the eastern Pacific, and is a powerful fighter when hooked.

The author has seen a tope taken aboard, and due to the trauma of capture, suddenly give birth to 20 or so live young. Anglers should bear in mind that it is only humane to get any fish that bears live young on capture back into the water as soon as possible.

Baits and fishing methods

This opportunistic predator will take whole fresh fish such as mackerel or herring, fish strips and squid. The best tackle is a 15kg class (30 lb) boat-rod and a reel loaded with wire line. Tope are fished for by the method known as the 'running ledger,' with weight and bait lying on the bottom.

Gummy shark

An IGFA-listed fish, the gummy shark (*Mustelus antarcticus*) is common in Australian and New Zealand waters. It does not have the formidable dentition of most sharks but its mouth has a mosaic of blunt teeth which it uses to crush crabs and shellfish, thus explaining its common name 'gummy'.

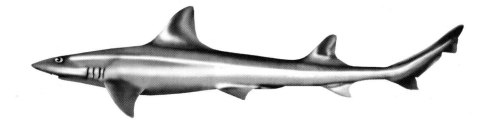

CHAPTER THREE

BAITS

Most of the saltwater big-game species that recreational anglers fish for are active predators that respond to in-built instinctive urges brought on by the need to evade other predators, capture food or reproduce.

The oldest truism in angling is that the best-ever, guaranteed-to-catch-fish bait cannot catch fish that are not there. With predatory fish the chances of catching them with a natural bait are often better than with an artificial bait such as a lure, spinner or fly, for if the offering is placed before them when they are in feeding mode, it is likely that they will take it. However, if they are not already feeding, the presence of either a natural or an artificial bait can often start them off.

The subject of baits is one that elicits a great deal of opinion but not much certainty. Why, for instance, do anglers catch salmon in rivers on artificial flies, lures, worms and shrimps, when this species has stopped feeding in the sea and entered freshwater for the sole purpose of breeding?

Likewise, what makes a particular species of game fish respond time and again to a specific lure or spinner, yet ignore a host of similar offerings.

Lists of baits that attract fish can be found in this and other how-to books, but on any given day a predatory fish might or might not take the particular bait offered it. Bait selection is not a science; much depends on the fish.

FISH AS BAIT

Live fishes make ideal bait for the obvious reason that they (and other forms of marine life such as crustaceans and molluscs) are the natural food of predatory fish. However, the use of live fish as bait is coming under fire from some factions who consider it cruel and there are many anglers who have stopped this practice. One scientific opinion has it that the nervous system of fish is not complex enough for them to experience pain as we know it. The decision must rest with each angler's con-

The protruding upper and lower jaws of sharks, including this shortfin mako (Isurus oxyrinchus), *enable them to bite large chunks of flesh, or even swallow their prey whole.*

science: is it more humane to kill the bait-fish first before putting it on the hook (and perhaps miss a fish), or should that blind instinct to kill be left to the predatory fish being sought?

There are some species of food-fish that are found in all the seas of the world, while others are confined either to one or both sides of the Atlantic, Indian, or Pacific oceans.

The list of fish that can be used dead or alive as hook-bait is very long, and some of the fish the big-game angler is prepared to put on a hook are big enough to be thoroughly welcomed by inshore anglers who are not accustomed to catching large fish.

Skippers will be aware of the location of shoals of bait-fish; where they are, so too will be the big-game species that feed on them. In general, the oily fish species are the most effective in attracting big-game fish; in the Atlantic these are the various mackerels and their close relatives, the Spanish and frigate mackerels, chub mackerel, herring, anchovy and pilchard and various mullets.

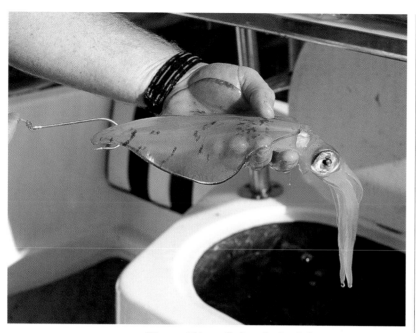

Live squid is readied on the hook for use as bait.

Always use a sturdy board when cutting up bait-fish.

MACKEREL

The mackerels belong to the Scombridae, the same family as the tunas and tunnies, but this does not stop the tunas from taking these tasty oily fish when they are offered as bait. All the marlins, too, will fall to a properly trolled mackerel. Live or dead, the mackerel is a fine bait.

The species most familiar to anglers on both sides of the Atlantic and in the Mediterranean is the Atlantic mackerel (*Scomber scombrus*).

The tropical and warm waters of the Pacific are home to the Spanish mackerel (*Scomberomorus maculatus*), also called the chub mackerel. Although there are other mackerels in the seas around Australia and New Zealand, they are probably the

Spanish or Pacific species under local names. The frigate mackerel (*Auxis thazard*) – also known as the frigate tuna – is smaller than the other mackerels, reaching weights of 3.1–3.6kg (7–8 lb). It is preyed upon by the blue marlin and so is an important bait for catching this species.

The horse mackerel (*Trachurus trachurus*) is another small fish used as bait in the North Atlantic, but its common name is misleading; it is actually one of the scads, which are recognized by a row of sharp scales along each flank, and can cause painful scratches when the fish is handled.

Big-game fish caught on mackerel: Atlantic and Pacific halibut, black marlin, blue marlin (usually on frigate mackerel), white marlin, jewfish, all the sharks. As with all the species below, although these big-game fish may favour certain baits, there can be no hard and fast rule that these are the only suitable bait-fish, and anglers should always experiment to find what works best for a particular time and place.

TUNA AND BONITO

Comparatively small tuna like the bonito, skipjack and frigate tuna (also called the frigate mackerel) are very useful baits for blue marlin and other large game fish, as they form part of their normal diet.

While the skipjack and dogtooth tuna are game fishes in their own right, the Atlantic bonito (*Sarda sarda*) can also be put on the hook as bait and trolled for the big-game fish. This is a fine example of a fish in the middle of the food chain, that is, both predator and prey.

When properly rigged for trolling, a small tuna will bounce and cavort through the waves very enticingly.

Big-game fish caught on tuna and bonito: marlin, swordfish, tuna, porbeagle and other sharks.

1. The hook size must fit the bait so that the bend is not too large for the depth of the fish.

2. Slit the fish from the vent to behind the gills and remove viscera and backbone.

3. Insert the hook so that a small part of the bend protrudes and the barb faces forward.

4. When the barb is positioned correctly, sew up the mouth with the line running out.

A small skipjack, or striped tuna, rigged as shark bait.

HERRING

Before commercial fishing caused fish populations to dwindle, herring shoals were considered to be limitless. While it is a useful hook-bait, the problem with the herring (*Clupea harengus*) is that, unlike the

Anglers use quiet periods to prepare fresh baits.

mackerel, it is rarely caught on rod and line or handline with feathers, so it usually has to be bought. Not quite so oily as mackerel, herring does not cut as nicely into strips, but it is certainly worth a try if a few can be bought from a just-berthed trawler.

The Pacific herring (*C. pallasi*) serves the same commercial purpose as the Atlantic species. Again, live herring are rare as bait-fish, so dead-baiting is usual. **Big-game fish caught on herring:** albacore, Atlantic and Pacific halibut, king mackerel, white marlin, swordfish, trevally, blackfin tuna, bluefin tuna, shark.

PILCHARD AND SPRAT

The pilchard (*Sardina pilchardus*) is a very oily little shoal-fish which, despite often being inaccurately described as the young of the herring, is actually an adult fish.

To compensate for its size, it is not unusual to put a bunch of them on the same hook. They are almost always used as a dead-bait.

The bait box is essential for tidiness.

The sprat (*Sprattus sprattus*), while not related to the pilchard, serves the same purpose, and is used in the same manner, especially for tope.

Both of these fish are prevalent in the eastern Atlantic, including around the Balearic and Canary islands, and in the Mediterranean. **Big-game fish caught on pilchard and sprat:** blue shark, tope and rays.

MULLET

The estuarine grey mullets familiar to European anglers are part of the family Mugilidae, but various species are found in all seas where big-game anglers pursue their sport. They are an ideal oily bait, whether they are used dead or alive.

A row of mackerel floating tantalizingly on a line.

Australian anglers record about 20 species, more than in any other part of the world. Local names for the grey mullet (*Mugil cephalus*) include striped, bully, hardgut, river and mangrove mullet.

Big-game fish caught on mullet: albacore, amberjack, dolphinfish, king mackerel, white marlin, tarpon, jewfish, bluefish and snook.

PINFISH

The pinfish (*Lagodon rhomboides*) is found from the Yucatán peninsula in Mexico, throughout the West Indies and up to Massachusetts on the US east coast. A member of the family Sparidae, it is a useful bait-fish because it is taken by game fish. About 30cm (1ft) long, it is mentioned only in the fish-bait lists of angling books.

Big-game fish caught on pinfish: amberjack, king mackerel and tarpon.

REDBAIT

The redbait (*Emmelichthys nitidus*) is so named because it appears to turn the sea red when it gathers in large shoals. In Australian waters it is called the red bait-fish, the red sea-harder, the picarel, the pearl fish and the red herring. In whimsical circles the last name might suggest it is unsuitable as a bait, but anglers will find this not so, for the species forms a large portion of the diet of barracuda and various of the tunas.

Big-game fish caught on redbait: barracuda, yellowfin tuna and blue marlin.

FLYING FISH

There are a number of species in the family Exocoetidae, which includes flying fish, the half-beaks and ballyhoo (described right). The tropical Atlantic species (*Exocoetus volitans* and *Cypselurus heterurus*), the Mediterranean species (*Hirundichthys rondeletil*) and the Indo-Pacific short-finned flying fish (*Parexocoetus brachypterus*) are all food of dolphinfish as well as bonito, which also has its own place in the food chain.

These fish do not fly, of course, but when evading predators such as dolphinfish, they skitter along the surface for distances of up to 183m (200yd), their pectoral fins vibrating.

Big-game fish caught on flying fish: black marlin, sailfish, bonito and dolphinfish.

Using their extended pectoral fins, flying fish skitter across the water, attracting bonito and dolphinfish.

BALLYHOO

The ballyhoo, or balao (*Hemiramphus brasiliensis*), is also known as the half-beak, because of the extreme length of its lower jaw. This is an important bait-fish in its home waters of the western Atlantic from Brazil to the Caribbean and Gulf of Mexico.

Big-game fish caught on ballyhoo: king mackerel, white marlin, sailfish, wahoo and dolphinfish.

NEEDLEFISH

Garfish, long toms and needlefish all belong to the family Belonidae, which includes the flying fishes and the half-beaks.

The needlefishes go under many names including skipjack (not the big-game species), saury, timucu, houndfish, agujon, barred long tom, silver gar and skipper.

These fish can be found in the waters of the West Indies, the eastern Atlantic, off Australia and in the eastern Pacific, where there are over a dozen species. They are edible and tasty, so do not be put off by the green bones.

Big-game fish caught on needlefish: tuna, king mackerel, swordfish and black marlin.

BAIT-FISH STRIP

The necessary tool for obtaining fish strip for hook-bait is a very sharp knife with a thin blade.

Two sizable strips (known as 'lask' or 'lash') will come from the flanks of a good-sized mackerel, probably the best of all fish species for its trolling properties, caused as oil droplets seep from the flesh, attracting game fish.

Slicing along the backbone, from the gill-cover towards the tail fin, will yield an ideal shape for the strip. When threaded onto the hook and trolled, the trail it leaves when moving through the water is one that no feeding predatory fish can ignore.

Big-game fish caught on fish strip: all species that take whole fish.

OTHER FORMS OF FISH BAIT

Cubing (chunking) involves using rough-cut pieces of the hook-bait to attract any predatory game fish that may be in the area.

If you are fishing for shark or any other eager species that are taken on fresh bait, when the strips have been removed for use as bait, the body of the fish, complete with head and entrails, can be put on the hook to leave an enticing trail of blood through the water while the boat trolls.

Big-game fish caught by cubing: all predatory fishes.

Care is needed when using the needlefish as bait.

Left *A few ballyhoo on a line can simulate the action of a small school.*

Marine worms attract rays and small shark that browse along the seabed.

MARINE WORMS

The marine worms most commonly used by anglers are the lugworm (*Arenicola marina*) – also known in the eastern Atlantic as the black lug or blow lug depending on size and bait-value – and the ragworm (*Nerisii spp*), larger specimens of which are known as king rag. They are mud and sand-dwellers and therefore not pelagic, but many fish usually found in blue water will take them avidly. An estimated 90 percent of all sea fish will accept marine worms as bait, good news for anglers, as worms require a great deal of patience to locate and catch. The ragworm, of which there are several species, is a formidable creature that can reach 0.6m (2ft) long and is equipped with bony pincers in the mouth capable of inflicting a painful (although not venomous) bite.

Big-game fishing is usually carried out with large fish-baits because the adage 'big bait for big fish' usually applies, but on the same hook, dangling attractively alongside the fish-bait, a couple of wriggling marine worms might well give that added interest to a feeding predator. A few canny anglers inject their marine worms with pilchard oil to increase the worms' attractiveness.

Big-game fishes caught with marine worms: rays, small shark and other predatory fish can be taken on the ragworm. Any big-game species that occur in shallow water, where they range about the seabed for food, will snap up wriggling marine worms.

SQUID, OCTOPUS AND CUTTLEFISH

These marine cephalopods are all predators themselves. They are characterized by the presence of a ring of prehensile tentacles around the mouth and form part of the large group of invertebrates (animals without backbones). Squid and octopus make fine bait, both whole and in pieces, and stay well on the hook (like all baits however, the fresher the better). Squid can often be bought frozen from supermarkets and fishmongers.

Small specimens can be used whole, while larger ones should have the head cut off, to be saved as bait, and the guts and cartilaginous bone removed.

If chumming is planned, the guts can go in the bin. The empty body-sac of the squid is then prepared for the hook by cutting the tentacles off and scraping away the coloured outer cuticle to expose the soft translucent flesh.

Big-game fish caught on squid, octopus and cuttlefish: swordfish, giant sea bass, bluefish, bonito, cobia, dolphinfish, halibut, marlin, sharks and tope.

COCKTAIL BAITS

Cocktail baits – a mixture of baits on one hook – seem to appeal to many fish species. It is due to their mixture of tastes or 'smells'. Try fish strip with an added squid tentacle; or fish strip with crab. Keep experimenting, as you never know which mixture will bring that special fish to the hook.

Big-game fish caught on cocktail baits: If any session seems to be fishless, this is the time for the cocktail bait; the species sought is immaterial.

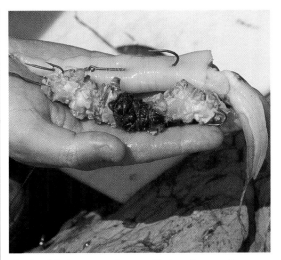

Cocktail baits are a mixture of baits whose various odours are designed to attract passing fish.

Below and below left *Squid, cuttlefish and octopus.*

1. Squid are a favourite food of most big-game fish. Lures often resemble the shapes and sizes of these cephalopods.

2. A high-speed bullethead lure like this can be effectively used to catch fast-moving species such as tuna and wahoo.

3. A medium-size Konahead lure, used for billfish and tuna. When trolled at high speed, the angled flat face of the lure creates a surface action and produces a long trail of bubbles.

4. The slim tapered head and large eyes of this medium-size lure resemble a baitfish or squid to a feeding marlin.

5. The umbrella-shaped nylon skirt, flashy head and large eyes of the 'Hawaiian Eye' lure produce a pulsating action on the surface that attracts barracuda, wahoo, tuna and billfishes.

6. A small Konahead rigged with trace and two hooks and sporting a multicoloured head and skirt combination.

7. A large slant-faced Kona lure for marlin. The roving eye and prism-foil head, combined with multicoloured skirts, are favoured by big-game fish. This lure has a 6m (19 ft) nylon trace and double shift rig hook for maximum hook-up ratios.

8. Chrome-headed lures are designed for high-speed trolling. The large lure has a hollow head and jet holes to allow water to be forced through under pressure, creating bubbles and noise to attract game fish.

ARTIFICIAL BAITS

Readers of angling publications and general fishing literature will be aware of the enormous importance some fly fishermen place on the colour of feathers and lures, while others insist that it is movement and action that attract the fish. The same applies to big-game angling.

To a feeding fish, lures, spinners, feathers, jigs and plugs are all potential food, even though their appearance to the human eye might suggest nothing more than a rather gaudy, totally unlifelike (and usually expensive) collection of feather, metal or man-made fibres. However, artificial baits, in whatever form, do catch fish.

LURES

There are many lures that regularly catch big fish and anglers assume that it is a combination of colour and action that triggers off a feeding response.

The Kona-type lures that are trolled on the surface have large, authentic-looking eyes set in a metal head, and tails in every colour imaginable. Why lures such as these, and the popular Rapala range, with the adjustable flap on the nose to give the lure a life-like action, should attract fish is uncertain – most of them exhibit very few features that suggest food-fish.

The popular Kona and Knucklehead lures originated in Hawaii and were at first made of wood; now they are made from plastics and come in a range of bright colours. Rapala, Iland and Sevenstrand are other well-known brands with large lifelike eyes. A variety of standard bodies is available and anglers have a wide choice of colourful nylon skirts with which to finish them off.

Big-game fish caught on lures: all species of pelagic, surface-feeding big-game fish will be attracted by the actions of a skittering, splashing, surface lure.

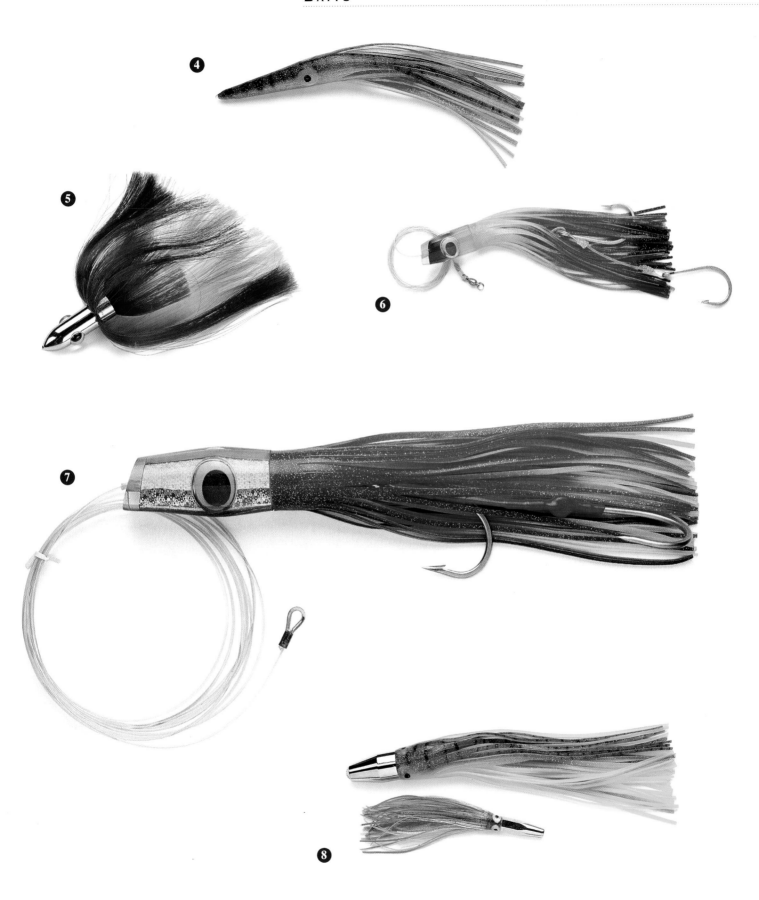

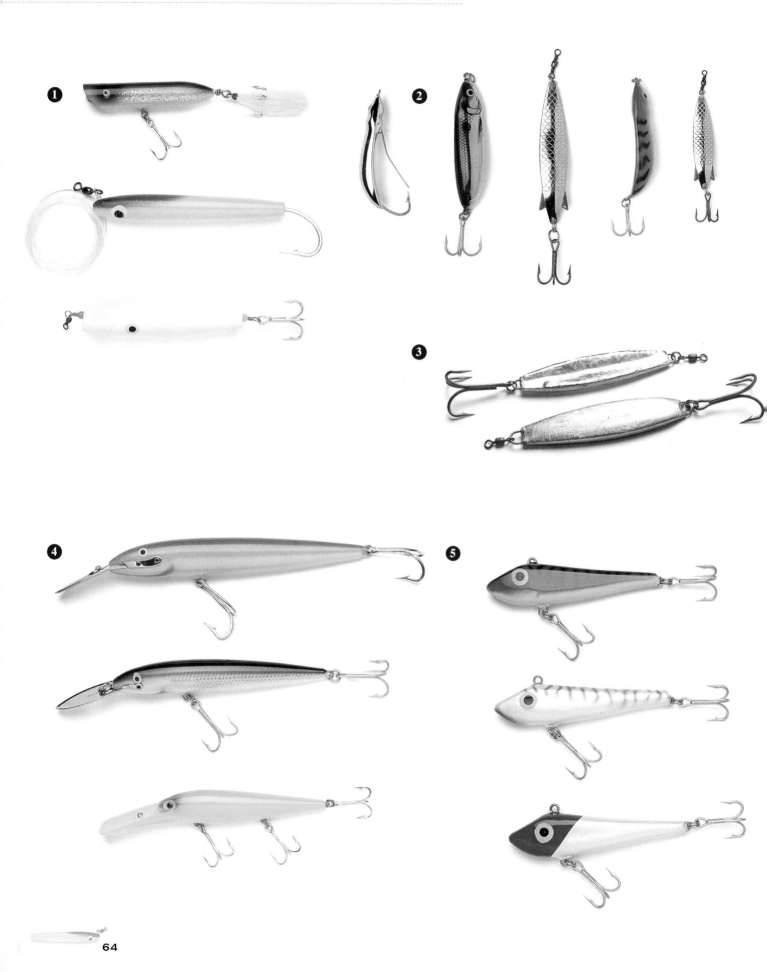

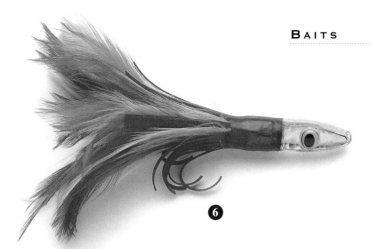

6

PLUGS

Among the artificial baits that have long and successful histories, plugs are to be seen ranged in tray after tray of colourful patterns in tackle shops. Of all the myriad lures, plugs bear the most resemblance to something animal, so they are favourite baits for anglers seeking the big predators; and are normally used to cast from a boat or for trolling. Some jointed models used to have up to three sets of treble hooks, but there are moves against this on the grounds of unnecessary cruelty. Plug size will depend on the species sought.

SPOONS

The spoon lure is so named because, long ago, a real spoon was fitted with a baited hook at one end and attached to the fishing line at the other, and it worked. These lures are possibly used more in freshwater angling, but there are bottom-fishing saltwater methods where they also work well

Most spoons have shiny, glittery curved bodies that shimmer and sparkle as they flutter through the water, giving the impression of sunlight on fish scales. Not all spoons have single or treble hooks; some are attached to the line about a foot above the hook, close to the last swivel, and when used this way they are known as attractor spoons.

Big-game fish caught on spoons: dolphinfish, tuna and larger mackerel-type fish.

JIGS

This is an obvious name, for the jig does just that when it is jerked about as the angler raises and lowers his rod-tip, imitating the darting movements of food-fish. Jigs, which usually provide their own weight, come in sizes to suit the fish being sought and can be used with or without a bait to attract some very large specimens. Jigs are popular off Australia's Great Barrier Reef .

PIRKS

The pirk is not one of the standard big-game baits or lures, for in reality it is a mite crude in its action, which is akin to the jig, but depends upon finding a shoal of fish and being drawn quickly upward and through them. In Norway, one kind of pirk which carried a number of treble hooks was so effective in pulling fish to the surface that it became known as the 'Ripper'. A modern version, not so be-rigged with trebles, has been named the 'Murderer'.

SPINNERS

Their name suggests their action, but this can become a pain in the neck when the line becomes twisted at the same time. Swivels help to avoid this, and there are anti-kink vanes that can be put on the last swivel to solve the problem.

As is the case with lures, spinners come in a variety of shapes and sizes and it is up to the angler to select the one that he feels will work best on the day. Like plugs, spinners can be either cast or trolled.

FEATHERS

Mackerel make a wonderful bait, but often just when you want to buy them, the fish trays are empty. Catch your own mackerel by using a light outfit and the standard line of six feathers. Not only is it entertaining (try controlling six healthy mackerel on those feathers as they try to swim in six different directions at once), but the fish could not be more fresh.

If there are mackerel in the water, the feathers will tempt them, and in half an hour at the most you will have all the fresh bait you need and some over for a tasty meal later.

When feathers are dry and in the tackle box, they look pretty useless as baits, but properly mounted on a long-shank hook and pulled through the water, they take on the actions and appearance of small, brightly coloured fish.

GROUNDBAIT/CHUM/BERLEY

These three words all refer to the same thing, depending on where you live: in the USA and South Africa it is chum, in Europe it is groundbait or rubby-dubby, and in Australia it is chum or berley. Whichever word is used, however, the concept is the same: a mixture of animal matter, often incorporating bran, bread, vegetable matter and 'secret' ingredients, put over the side of the boat to attract fish to the baited hook either from the surface or from the seabed where some species feed. To avoid repetition, in this section it is called GCB.

A frequent cause of uncontrollable nausea in anglers is when the container is first opened and some of the contents thrown overboard: but this soon turns to sudden cure and elation when it works, and large big-game fish are hooked!

There is a tradition in European circles that GCB should consist of a large drum full of very old fish remains (usually scraped up from the fish well), fish heads and entrails from the gutting floor of the local fish-market, all thoroughly mashed up with fish oil, then stood in the sun for a day or two. However, only the angler lacking any olfactory sense would be able to assist the skipper or deckhand to remove the lid and pour the contents into the sea. While the author has been present when this has been effective, the considered opinion of big-game anglers in other parts of the world, especially Australia, is that the most foul-smelling mixture is not necessarily the most attractive GCB as far as the fish are concerned.

Another way to introduce GCB to the water is to fill a sack or fine-mesh net with it, hang it over the side and allow the motion of the boat to knock it

against the side and release particles and scent, or to hit the bag at intervals to achieve the same result. The author has witnessed the use of a gigantic homemade 'bait-dropper' filled with GCB and lowered to the seabed.

It must be added here that in its regulations, the International Game Fish Association states very clearly that the use of GCB will negate any claim for a rod-caught record fish. This is not looked on at all favourably by many fishing bodies, the Australians in particular disagreeing with the principle of banning something they see as a quite legitimate ploy in angling for big-game fish.

Chum is a mixture of chopped bait-fish, innards and blood released into the sea to attract big-game fish.

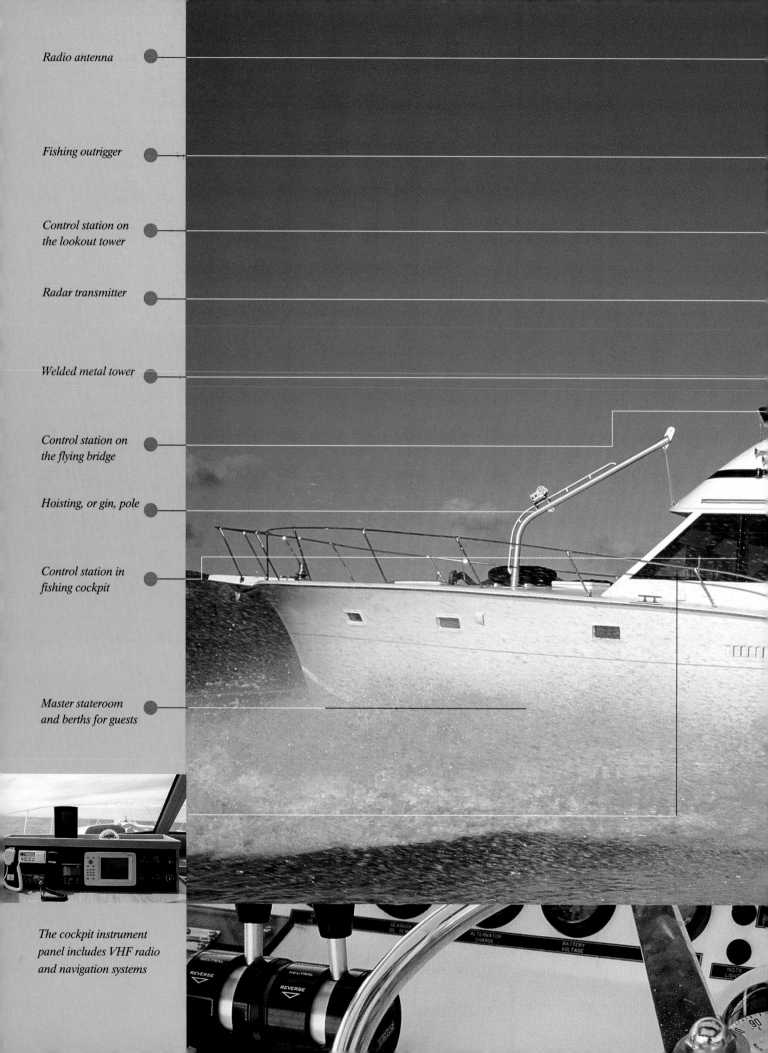

Radio antenna

Fishing outrigger

Control station on
the lookout tower

Radar transmitter

Welded metal tower

Control station on
the flying bridge

Hoisting, or gin, pole

Control station in
fishing cockpit

Master stateroom
and berths for guests

The cockpit instrument
panel includes VHF radio
and navigation systems

Ladder leading to the
flying bridge

Rod holding station

Fighting chair

Tackle station with
preparation area, bait
board and bait freezer

CHAPTER FOUR

BOAT EQUIPMENT AND SAFETY

Take a walk along the quay at any dock or marina in one of the world's game-fishing centres, and you will be confronted by some of the sleekest, slickest craft on the water.

Deep-sea angling for big-game fish such as marlin and broadbill is not for the impoverished, and many 'ordinary' anglers are grateful for the opportunity to crew on one of these magnificent vessels.

However, with more and more big-game anglers considering the acquisition of their own craft, the question is, what should one look for in a boat in which fishing is the prime reason for ownership?

BOATS

The first step – to decide what kind of fishing you are after – is often dictated by location. The kind of species sought, the waters in which you will be fishing, the total number of people who will fish with you, launching facilities and how long you are likely to be at sea, are all factors to take into account before you start reading manufacturers' brochures.

Cost is, of course, a vital factor, unless your personal finances are bottomless, in which case you can simply employ a top-class expert to advise you on a suitable craft and all you have to do is write the cheques. But for the angler not in that category, you want the right craft at the right price, and one which will enable you to do your fishing in safety and in the knowledge that it will get you back to base. Don't buy a boat, however just because it sounds cheap or the price is all you can afford – you might be faced with very large bills for repairs.

A good first step would be to write around, asking for brochures to give you an idea of the craft currently for sale and the sort of money involved.

Deep-sea craft such as these are found in most of the world's top game fishing locations.

Angling journals and boating magazines all carry boat offers, but don't believe all you read – like property advertisements, 'needs renovation' probably covers a multitude of horrors. Even if the offer does appear to describe just the boat you are looking for, it's a good idea to obtain the help of an expert to check it over for you, just as you should when buying another car or second home. Buying a boat is, in fact, very much like buying a car. Don't be taken in by that cheerful salesman who points out all the pluses but omits to explain why the engine mounts are loose, a couple of the instruments don't work, some of the fittings are not corrosion-proof, there are a few mysterious dents in the keel and the rudder squeaks. (Paintwork can be a pointer – if it is very fresh, it might be hiding something.)

The fisherman will want good dry stowage in his boat for fishing and safety gear, vertical or horizontal supports for rods, fishing stations with adequate deck room, a fish-well to hold the catch to be retained as food or bait, a bait-cutting table, gaffs with extendible handles, the facilities and equipment for making hot drinks, a fridge or coldbox to hold food and cold drinks, and a lavatory with a door.

BOAT SIZE

When making your selection, the size of boat chosen will depend on how you intend to get it to the water. A 9m (30ft) cabin craft with either a big inboard or an outboard motor requires a permanent berth, and often there are long waiting lists at popular harbours and marinas. For the smaller craft, in the 4.8m (16ft) range and perhaps slightly longer, loading the boat onto a trailer by means of a hand-turned winch should be reasonably easy.

The boat must sit securely on the trailer and your car must have sufficient power to pull both trailer and boat along comfortably, not only on the flat but up and down hills, as well as back up the slipway after the boat has been loaded. Off-road or four-wheel-drive vehicles are ideal as they are built for this kind of strenuous work.

MATERIALS

In the past boats were made always of wood. This changed in the early 19th-century, when Scotsman John Laird began using iron for shipbuilding. The first Ironclad, built in 1859, proved that even a large ship made of iron will float if it is the right shape. Although some rowing-boat-sized hulls are still made of wood, man-made materials like aluminium, plastic, fibreglass, Kevlar and other 'space-age' compounds are preferred.

When it comes to money, the angler who has bought a rod made from Kevlar will be well aware that it costs more than rods made from other substances, and the same applies to boats. Made by DuPont, Kevlar is an aromatic polyamide fibre of great strength. It was first used in tyre manufacture and for bullet-proof body protection. The attraction of Kevlar lies in its strength/weight ratio, which is better than aluminium.

HULL

The kind of hull your boat needs will depend on the fishing you have in mind. A flat-bottomed hull is fine for shallow, inshore waters, but take it out into a sea with any waves and you will be uncomfortable.

In any case, the big-game fishermen needs a craft that can get out into blue water where the swordfish and the marlin play, and one that will be able to cope safely with most conditions created by wind and water (this is a serious matter, as the sea can be calm one minute, a killer the next).

The V-shaped hull, of which there are many variations, gives a good motion through the waves. The initial design was a very shallow V (almost a 'ghost keel') which gave improved stability. A deeper V was followed by the modified V, then the addition of trim planes (attached to each side of the hull below the waterline), which gave an even smoother ride, all these changes being designed to improve a boat's stability. Last came the tri-hull, also called the 'cathedral hull', which is even more stable and – important in angling terms – which rides well on the drift and at anchor out at sea.

Not apparent at first with the tri-hull is the gaining of space, as the overall shape of the hull is more or less rectangular and thus offers more cubic feet. Apart from splashing anglers more than usual, this shape both handles and sits well in choppy water.

ENGINES

If the boat you select comes complete with an engine, either inboard or stern-attached, the accompanying handbook (don't forget to ask for it!) will provide all the details of engine handling, power output, basic mechanics and the speed at which your boat will take you out to the fishing grounds.

If your boat does not have a power plant, you will have to purchase one. If you are knowledgeable about engines, this is where you can save money. On the other hand, you may be the best sportfisherman in the country but a total ignoramus when it comes to engines – in this case, you will have to pay for professional advice (unless you live next door to an engine expert and offer to take him out fishing in return for some pointers).

A rough guide to engine size is that for a fishing boat of up to 6m (20ft) long you will need an engine of some 80HP to take you out a good distance.

The deep 'V' hull (top), double hull (centre) and tri-hull (bottom) are used by boat-builders around the world.

A Volvo inboard diesel engine (top) *and a Honda 4-stroke 75HP outboard motor* (bottom).

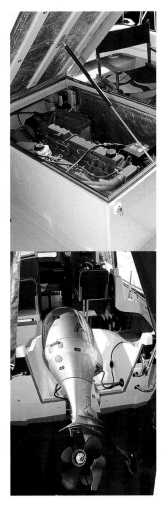

Sport anglers and commercial fishermen often work the same waters, not always harmoniously.

Anglers do not lounge about on deck enjoying the view; they are busy preparing terminal rigs, cutting up bait or checking hook points – all actions which need room. This is the advantage of the inboard engine, which is either confined in a stout engine cover or built down into the hull, leaving good deck space.

Points to take into consideration are repairs and maintenance and, more importantly, replacement. Removing an inboard engine from a boat is a major, usually costly, exercise.

Your boat should come with papers or bear a notice about the maximum horsepower (HP) advised for it. If you ignore this advice and install a more powerful motor, you might get a few more knots out of it, but if you have problems which involve injury to others followed by litigation, you might find yourself on the losing side if the engine has more horsepower than it should.

Inboard–Outboard Motors

An inboard motor, which drives the propeller through a shaft, powers many mid-range fishing boats. Situated in the centre and slightly abaft, it is easy to access and maintain. A liability of the inboard motor is its weight, but then an outboard has still to be transported on the trailer.

On smaller boats the outboard motor is ideal. It gives more room on board, is portable and the hinged mounting is useful over snags.

The best of both worlds is, however, the inboard-outboard. Designed to offer the advantage of a permanently installed motor in the centre-hull, it also comes with the benefits of an outboard, with its great ability to manoeuvre the craft without the linkages of steering wheels and wiring which can fail at the wrong moment. The hinged prop and shaft can be lifted clear of obstacles in the water.

GETTING YOUR SKIPPER'S TICKET

Craft that are capable of going long distances out to sea and staying there for days cannot be handled without the proper training and certification. It is not enough to be able to steer straight for a visible mark, shut down and begin drift-fishing, or reduce power and start trolling. Various certification courses are available, all of which cover basics such as boat handling (including power-boat manoeuvres and short sea passages), blind pilotage, navigation and the use of electronic equipment, mooring, anchor work and safety at sea.

A yachtmaster's course, taken in collaboration with a VHF radio certificate and first-aid certificate, is the most commonly available training. Details can normally be obtained from your local boat club or marina.

Other useful courses cover fire-fighting at sea, survival, distress and safety systems, and radar and navigational aids, all of which aid one's competence in taking fully equipped boats to sea. If you carry paying passengers, you will need to be properly insured.

The sportfisherman boat design originated in Florida, USA, but is now seen throughout the world.

THE SPORTFISHERMAN DESIGN

This type of boat was designed in the USA specifically for big-game fishing and is now popular worldwide. It comes in various sizes, from an impressive 12m-plus (40ft-plus) down to 7.6m (25ft). First appearing 30 years ago, when the diminishing number of big-game fish was becoming accepted, these craft are able to seek the big-game species away from the traditional areas that in many cases have been over-fished. In the area where the sportfisherman design originated – the seas off Florida – the wanderings of big-game fish species meant that anglers seeking them had to be prepared to follow the fish over long distances, in boats able to cope with variable, and often-unpredictable, weather conditions.

The sportfisherman is not a trade name but a generic design. The angler fortunate enough to order one can include any fishing aid he wants, his only limitation being the cost. The big top of the range models are equipped with everything: fighting seats, outriggers, a flying bridge, a functional galley, sleeping accommodation, and a spar called a gin-pole which is necessary when you hook that record blue marlin and can't haul its 589.5kg (1300 lb) bulk aboard. These boats are usually permanently moored, although smaller versions can be towed to the water on trailers.

EQUIPMENT

Most boats specifically designed for big-game fishing have a variety of equipment geared towards making it easier for the angler to find and to fight the fish.

FIGHTING SEATS

A fighting seat (or fighting chair) holds the angler steady on the boat while he is playing something far stronger than himself, which might otherwise pull him over the side. Without it, the biggest game fish would simply run all the line off the reel and then break free. The chair enables the angler to place his feet on the foot-rest and use the strength in his legs and arms to combat the pull of the fish. The first pulls will indicate the size and strength of the fish, and if it is something special, straps will be clipped onto the reel, with the rod butt already in the gimbal

The fighting chair assists anglers, but if a record is to be claimed, there are IGFA regulations governing its use.

in addition to the fighting chair. The simplest form of aid in fighting a strong fish is the use of a rod-butt holder, also called a cup, bucket or gimbal which, fixed to a leather pad, is worn round the waist. The butt-end of the rod fits into this and acts as a fulcrum while the angler uses both hands on the rod.

The fighting harness is an elaboration of this simple butt-holder and consists of shoulder straps, or a kidney harness, with a strap which clips onto the reel. Thus the rod is secured in the butt cap or gimbal by the reel, allowing the angler to concentrate on playing the fish without fear of the rod being pulled from his hands and without having his movements constricted by a fighting chair.

OUTRIGGERS

Outriggers are those long poles made of aluminium, fibreglass, wood, bamboo and a variety of other materials, that can be seen extending from the sides of big-game boats. Designed to keep up to four lines (and therefore up to four baits or lures) well spaced and in the chosen position for trolling or drifting; outriggers also prevent too much pressure being put on the rod-tip while trolling; and they take the strain off the angler's arms.

Above and below *Outriggers keep the lines clear of the boat. When entering or leaving port they are stowed upright.*

in front of the seat. The angler can then concentrate on controlling the reel with the lever drag until the spool can be locked and reeling in begins.

Fighting seats could be said to 'assist' the angler, and for IGFA purposes they must not have any appliance or mechanism that aids an angler in fighting a fish. If he or the skipper senses that a new record might be in the vicinity, the angler may use the seat (and a harness, see next section) but the latter must not be attached to the seat.

There are many kinds of fighting chairs, from the portable seat which cannot swivel to the type that is a permanent, swivelling fixture on the boat, and has an adjustable footrest and attached rod-butt holder. If your boat is big enough for a fighting chair, go for a model that needs the minimum of attention and get expert advice on the installation if you are unsure.

FIGHTING HARNESSES

A desire to make playing a big-game fish more of an equal-opportunity struggle between man and beast gave rise to the fighting harness, which is often used

In large charterboats, outriggers as long as 9m (30ft), support the trolled bait during the fishing session and until a target fish takes the bait. They must also be capable of folding back for docking otherwise the outriggers could well foul other boats or any quayside obstruction, causing damage.

IGFA regulations for record purposes require that the line be attached to a snap (or clip, rather like a fold-back or bulldog clip) by a release device that comes into operation on a sharp pull from a taking fish, so that the angler can then take over.

FLYING BRIDGE

When standing on a normal bridge, one's view of the surrounding ocean can be limited, so that signs of big-game fish on or near the surface can be missed and possible sport from that sighting lost. Twenty or

Above *A lookout tower improves fish-sighting possibilities.*

more years ago, some skippers manufactured a crude structure from pipes, which stood considerably higher than the normal bridge. While one person controlled the boat, another climbed a ladder to the crude platform and had a much better view of the sea. The next step was to install engine controls and a wheel so that the craft could be operated from above. Any fishing boat can be fitted with a flying

bridge, but care must be taken to allow for the change in the craft's centre of gravity. All sportfisherman type boats now incorporate a flying bridge. Another version of the flying bridge is the 'tuna tower', used first in 1952 for the obvious purpose of sighting tuna. The height of the tower, which is made of aluminium tubing, depends on the length of the boat and its stability, the height being half of the craft's length.

RADAR REFLECTORS

Radar reflectors are vital on small boats that may not show up on ships' radar screens in waves of some size. Fishing boats that go into blue water should always hang radar reflectors high on the mast, as these metal structures, situated well above wave height, will then create a blip on the radar screens of nearby ships, warning them of the presence of a sizeable object.

Of course, you should never drift or anchor in a busy shipping lane – it is not unknown for large commercial vessels to steam on autopilot through a channel without keeping much of a lookout.

ELECTRONIC AIDS

Deep-sea anglers have access to a wide range of hi-tech electronic aids such as fish-finders, depth-sounders, navigation aids and position indicators that were unknown a few decades ago.

Possibly the most important electronic aid in fishing terms, depending on what the finances will stand, is the **fish-finder**. This instrument operates a transducer, which provides the angler with a profile of the seabed over which he is moving.

A **magnetometer,** which measures the intensity or direction of a magnetic field, can pinpoint wrecks, which are often a home for all kinds of fish upon which the big predators feed.

The **digital thermometer,** another useful instrument, will give you a constant indication of the ambient water temperature at the surface, giving a simple reading on a small box in the wheelhouse. Some big-game fish species, such as tarpon, barracuda and marlin, prefer water temperatures in the 15-30°C (59-86°F) range, while swordfish and albacore prefer cooler water. Therefore knowing the temperature of the water may indicate whether the fish you are seeking is likely to be found in the vicinity.

NAVIGATION AIDS

There was a time when experienced skippers would steam out on a time-and-tide basis, and very skilfully drop anchor or begin the drift exactly at the right mark. Since then, science has made things easier.

Thanks to satellite technology, by using the appropriate electronic aids the deep-sea angler can tell to within a few metres exactly where he is. Hand-held navigation instruments show your precise position and can even plot your position in relation to pre-installed charts. These use a minimum of three satellites, so being lost at sea is becoming rare. If the batteries unexpectedly run down, an emergency internal back-up system comes into play.

There are a number of global positioning systems (GPS's) in use around the world which use satellite navigation to enable anglers to determine their position with absolute accuracy. An additional, useful asset of GPS is the ability to rendezvous with other craft at sea while avoiding complex traditional navigation methods.

While all these aids are wonderful, if they fail (which they can do), it is up to the skipper to undertake any navigation necessary, so a compass and the relevant charts must be to hand at all times.

FISH FINDERS

Sonar played a large part in anti-submarine warfare. Now it is used by anglers not only to help in locating individual fish but to inform them of how deep the fish are swimming. The fish-finder shows individual fish hovering over wrecks or reefs. The same kind of equipment gives an accurate, detailed profile of the seabed as the boat passes over it. Wrecks and other obstacles, and their depths, can be easily identified, and are obvious places for fish to congregate and feed on the smaller food-fish.

The most expensive fish-finders come complete with printers to give a permanent record, and a sensitivity-adjustment feature that can show fish shoals, and even individual specimens if they are big enough. Portable fish-finders are also available.

COMPASS

If you intend to go beyond sight of land, as most big-game anglers do, you must be able to find your way back to port if all your electronics fail. This is where a compass becomes useful.

A compass works through the earth's magnetism and is affected by nearby metals, such as the boat's engine. Mount the compass as far away from it as possible, preferably near the navigation instruments so that you can monitor them at the same time.

Bear in mind that a compass needle points to magnetic north and not true north. While this has a minimal effect on navigation over a few miles, it can lead to much larger errors as distances increase. Keep notes of the course you take out and the strength of the tide, both out and in, and be aware that steering a straightforward reciprocal course when heading for home will probably not get you there, because tide and wind will collaborate to affect the direction in which you are heading. In unfamiliar waters, try and have a panoramic photo of the port area on board to refer to on your return.

The instrument panels house the compass and radio, as well as a variety of navigation aids and fish finders.

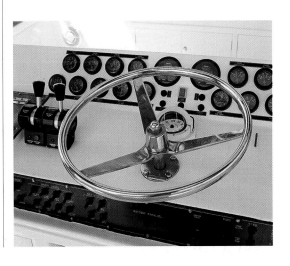

The engine instruments above the wheel show temperature, revs, fuel and oil pressure.

RADIO

There are many reasons for having a VHF marine radio aboard – weather news, distress ('mayday') calls to coastguards, ship-to-ship chatter (which should be kept to a minimum to avoid blocking important radio traffic), and even for leisure listening if the fish are ignoring you. Correct radio procedure is vital, and for that you must take the proper courses of tuition, followed by an examination. You will need a licence before you can transmit on VHF.

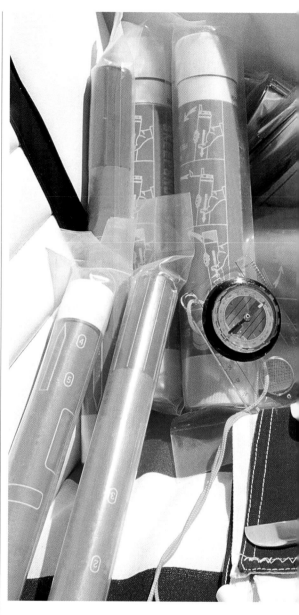

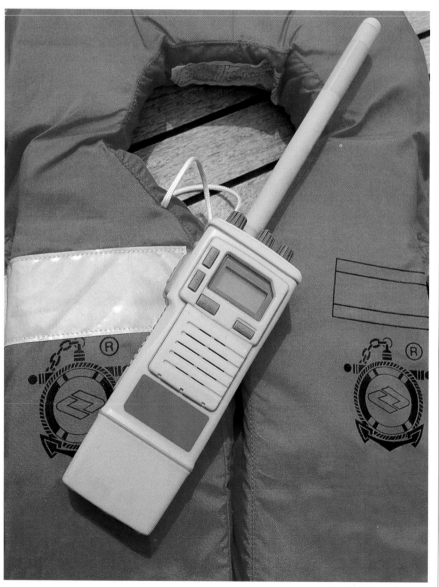

Only a foolhardy skipper would put to sea without minimum safety equipment, such as a life jacket and hand-held VHF marine radio.

SAFETY

Safety is an important concern for anyone putting to sea, but particularly for anglers venturing into deep waters beyond the sight of land.

While the ultimate responsibility rests with the skipper, all anglers aboard should know where the safety equipment is located and how to operate it in an emergency.

Safety regulations may differ from country to country and anglers chartering boats away from home should ensure that they are aware of the local rules and regulations.

optimum height; enabling the glowing flare to sink slowly downwards, giving a great deal more time for it to be seen. Keep in mind that flares have an expiry date, so check the packaging before you buy them.

Fire extinguishers

A fire at sea when you are some way from land is both frightening and dangerous. When you buy a fire extinguisher, make sure you read the instructions on how to use it properly, and practise doing so (without actually setting it off!). Where there are engines there is also electricity, so the boat owner must carry fire extinguishers that can cope with electrical fires. The number of extinguishers will depend on the size of the boat, but a minimum of two is necessary to avoid disaster if the only one on board fails to operate.

Hooters

If your ship-to-shore radio packs up, waving your arms and shouting may attract the necessary attention if the nearest boat is only 90m (100 yd) away. If not, things could become awkward. Some kind of noise-making device is a useful item to have on board. Whistles operated by high-pressure air work well, but the best noise-maker is a foghorn-type hooter, the sound of which carries well over water.

There are a number of internationally recognized signals of distress, such as a four-second blast every two minutes, or the setting off of flares. Of course, the skipper of any craft in the vicinity of another that is sending out hooter noises (or sending up flares) will head towards the other boat to see if assistance is required.

Above A fire on board is a serious matter. Always carry at least two fire extinguishers, and ensure that you know how to use them.
Below *Hooters attract attention in a crisis as their sound carries well across water.*

Flares

Red and orange are the best smoke colours for their visibility at sea and against any kind of sky. Basic safety regulations recommend that you carry two flares for trips close to shore and up to 4,8km (3 miles) out; eight flares, including parachute flares for up to 11km (7 miles); and 10, including four parachute flares, if you are heading out more than 11km. US Coastguard regulations require a minimum of three flares to be carried at all times. As the name suggests, parachute flares include a small canopy which opens when the flare reaches

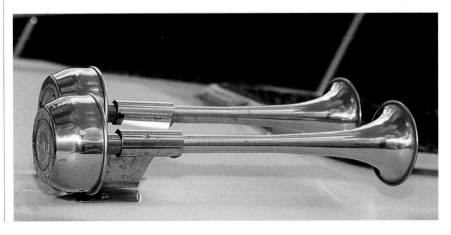

The fighting chair or seat helps the angler to subdue and reel in a big-game fish that may weigh substantially more than he or she does.

GENERAL EQUIPMENT

ANCHORS

The author has fished from boats which used large, odd-shaped boulders as anchors which, while effective in shallow water, were not very nautical, nor were they officially approved anchors, which are obligatory on all sea-going boats.

Close inshore is not the normal fishing area for the blue-water angler, whose fishing marks are usually well beyond anchoring depth. Yet an anchor can be very useful in slowing down a rate of drift in wind that is coming from the wrong direction. For this purpose a length of heavy chain is just as good, or a heavy stone or metal ball on the end of the chain, but nonetheless, a proper anchor appropriate to your craft is a must. It must be heavy enough to hold the boat steady, but not so bulky that its weight badly affects the boat's movement when running at sea.

One important point: a single anchor is not enough for any sea angling boat. Lose it, and you can be in serious trouble if the wind is blowing you offshore, or worse, toward rocks.

When fishing at anchor, the boat can be moved by wind-plus-current, or wind-against-current. Either can be frustrating for the angler, who usually wants the boat to stay over a wreck or some particular mark. If the anchor rope is attached to the boat from both the bow and the stern, forming a V shape, much unwanted swing can be avoided.

Mechanical anchors

These may or may not have flukes (the pointed barbs on the anchor arms); some have three, others four arms. The anchor must lie flat on the seabed and be capable of being held there by its weight. Between the anchor-head and the rope

there should be 4.5m (14ft) or so of substantial chain, which aids in keeping the anchor-head down. The old, traditional anchor has passed the test of time, but modern designs include an anchor trip – an additional line attached to the rope – which is very useful if it snags on an obstruction.

Sea anchors

Sometimes called drogues or drift-anchors, sea anchors fulfil two very important functions: they hold the boat into the wind when drifting, and help keep it off rocks if it is being blown close to them. Sea anchors are commonly cone-shaped and made of sacking or similar material. The cone is filled with water and acts as a brake to the boat's movements. In an emergency, a bucket on a rope can be used.

The anchor buoy

When anchoring, always attach a marker buoy to the rope, then connect that to the boat. This allows you to free the anchor in a hurry, without having to haul it up from the seabed. The anchor buoy (which must be able to stay afloat on the surface even if the anchor is suspended) will mark the anchor's position for when you return.

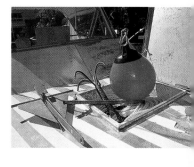

An anchor accompanied by its marker buoy.

Anchors come in various styles, but all serve the same purpose – to hold the boat in a specific position. When not in use, the anchor should be safely stowed, but must always be easily accessible if required in a hurry.

Knives, scissors and specialized tools for removing hooks should always be safely stowed when not in use.

FISH CONTAINERS

Those big fish you have caught have to be kept out of the water if you don't want some hungry shark to come along and dine on your prize catch. If your boat is large enough, a container can be inserted into a recess in the transom. It will take all average-sized fish whether you want to use them as bait or for taking home for supper. These containers should be metal (zinc) lined and have some drainage; certain models with grids allow the sea to flush through the container and keep the fish fresh. Others are kept below deck, with access through a hatch. Portable containers can also be hung over the side.

Obviously, containers are not big enough for the very large big-game fish. Should the angler hook something the size of his boat and subdue it, his day's fishing will probably be over, for he must lash the fish to the side, or tow it, and head for home.

KNIVES

Most anglers have their favourite bait-cutting knife, usually one with an extremely sharp blade, kept in a leather sheath with a fastener and often worn on a belt round the waist. The most suitable knives are buoyant and will float if accidentally dropped overboard. Care must be exercised when using bait knives in rough seas as a sudden lurch of the boat, at the moment an angler prepares to slice open a fish on the bait-board, might quite unintentionally cause serious injury. All boats should have first-aid equipment on hand for this kind of emergency.

BILGE-PUMP

In the days when fishing boats were made of wood, bilge-pumps were a vital necessity. These days, with hulls made from dependable manmade materials, the bilge-pump is needed only when sea water starts to slop over the sides. Even that is largely avoided if slots at deck level allow the water to run off as soon as it washes aboard. Sea water penetrating into the well of an inboard engine can cause its failure. This is where the bilge-pump earns its place.

BALERS

You may consider a baler something of a quaint idea, but if your small boat is holed or develops a leak where it is difficult to insert a plug, and you do not have a bilge-pump fitted, you will be glad of it.

The bilge pump comes into its own if sea water inadvertently enters the engine compartment or other below-deck space.

CAMERAS

Although not a necessary part of a fishing boat's equipment, if you hook and boat a record-breaker and there's not a camera in sight, you'll curse everything and everyone on board. Charterboat skippers often have camcorders or cameras ready because the photographs make good publicity for them.

Replacing a camera lost overboard can be expensive, so include all cameras in your insurance policy.

Remember that if your camera is lost or damaged on a fishing trip, the insurance company may demand proper witness statements.

INSURANCE

This may seem like an unusual topic to include, but if you are a boat-owner the subject should be familiar to you. A boat, trailer and all the related fishing equipment and gear are valuable properties and, since they are comparatively portable, they can attract the attention of thieves.

Take out adequate insurance for yourself, your boat, its contents and trailer, and your tackle – and don't go for the cheapest offer. There are excellent firms which specialize in marine insurance. (Since prevention is always better than cure, never leave expensive, easily removable items on the boat, whether it is at home or on a permanent mooring.)

Boats taking anglers out professionally must have covering passenger insurance. There will be evidence of it on board; don't be afraid to ask about it.

SAFETY AT SEA

When a big fish is hooked, the excitement can create so much euphoria on board – not only for the angler with the rod but in those around him – that safety can be overlooked. Respect for the sea in all its many moods is vital for anyone who participates in watersports of any type. A person can drown in a flat, calm sea just as easily as in waves 3m (10ft) and more high, and no angler should become so confident that 'safety first' is forgotten.

If a deep-sea fishing boat is doing anything other than bobbing quietly in a motionless sea, someone must be aware at all times of where everyone is, especially when a fish breaks the surface for the first time. In a small craft, if everyone crowds to one side and leans over, it doesn't take much to create a pronounced heel and a sudden loss of balance, with potentially disastrous consequences.

Knowing where you are

Deep-sea anglers have at least one duty in common with hikers, hill-walkers, mountaineers and cavers (in fact, anyone whose sport of choice comes with a touch of danger), and that is to make sure that those back on land know more or less what direction they are heading in and roughly when they are due back. Responsible skippers sign out when they leave port and check in on their return. They also advise their local port control office if they are moving off to seek new fishing grounds.

Listening to the skipper

On-board, the ultimate responsibility rests with the skipper. If he has heard of deteriorating weather and says, 'Reel in, we're heading back,' this is not a suggestion, it is an order, and one which must be accepted no matter how big the fish are or how eager the anglers are to continue fishing.

A change in the weather can prolong a return journey, particularly if you are running into the wind, and the skipper will take this and other factors into account when calling it a day.

If you are taking out a boat without its usual crew, someone proficient in boat-handling and VHF radio must be among the party.

WEATHER

Weather is a fact of life for anglers, who should always be aware of weather changes and listen to forecasts even when not planning a trip out.

The keen angler will buy a book on simple meteorology to help him understand a bit about weather maps. An on-going interest in weather enables the angler to make his own decisions and these, coupled with the official broadcasts, will be enough for foward planning. Radio stations issue regular weather forecasts based on satellite information transmitted on a global basis and most areas offer constantly updated weather information over the telephone.

Understanding simple weather charts is not difficult. Two main frontal systems are the high-pressure area and the low-pressure area (air masses tend to move from high to low pressure). A high pressure forecast usually indicates good clear skies, but it also can bring strong winds; whereas low-pressure might mean cloudy skies and rain.

The internationally recognized Beaufort Scale, which measures wind velocity, divides weather conditions into 12 categories, from calm to hurricane force.

A skipper may decide to head for home based on his judgement of prevailing weather conditions, the depth of the sea below the boat (which affects wave height), how the craft behaves in heavy seas or high winds and the distance between the fishing grounds and home port.

BEAUFORT SCALE

WEATHER	WIND SPEED	WAVE HEIGHT
Force 0	Under 1 knot	None
Calm. Mirror-like sea.		
Force 1	1–3 knots	About 0.07m (3in)
Light air. Rippled sea.		
Force 2	4–6 knots	About 0.15m (6in)
Light breeze. Short waves, crests do not break.		
Force 3	7–10 knots	About 0.6m (2ft)
Gentle breeze. Large wavelets, crests starting to break.		
Force 4	11–16 knots	0.9–1.2m (3–4ft)
Moderate breeze. Waves much longer, white horses.		
Force 5	17–21 knots	1.8m (6ft)
Fresh breeze. Waves bigger, spray starting.		
Force 6	22–27 knots	2.7–3m (9–10ft)
Strong breeze. Very large waves with extensive crests, much spray.		
Force 7	28–33 knots	4–4.2m (13–14ft)
Near gale. Sea heaping up, white foam blown in streaks in the direction of the wind.		
Force 8	34–40 knots	5.5m (18ft)
Gale. High, long waves, spindrift, foam blown in large streaks in the direction of the wind.		
Force 9	41–47 knots	7m (23ft)
Strong gale. High waves, wave crests topple and tumble over, spume blown by wind.		
Force 10	48–55 knots	8.8m (29ft)
Storm. Very high waves, surface white, sea violent, very poor visibility.		
Force 11	56–63 knots	11m (37ft)
Violent storm. Medium-sized vessels disappear in troughs, sea covered in foam, extremely poor visibility.		
Force 12	64+ knots	Over 11m (37ft)
Hurricane. Sea a maelstrom.		

Regular anglers should buy some items of specialized clothing that have been designed to cope with wet, and often cold, conditions.

CLOTHING

Every angler will pick his clothing to suit the conditions in which he is fishing. Winter fishing in cold waters requires a whole range of specialized protective gear, from full-body oilskins to weatherproof jackets, warm hats and gloves.

However, even in balmy climates in which the need for anything other than a T-shirt and a pair of shorts seems ludicrous, it is vital to have a sweater or warm top in your pack. If you fall overboard, all it will take is a light breeze to chill you.

Never assume the day will remain fine and the sunshine continuous; always be prepared for the unexpected chilly wind or squall. That sweater or windcheater packed into a travel-bag can make all the difference between feeling comfortable and shivering. Anglers going out for a full day might include long trousers or sweatpants and dry shoes, or even a full change of clothing if a few drinks in the pub afterwards are in order.

Many angling clubs have well-equipped ablution facilities with hot showers, so keep a spare towel in your bag as well.

Footwear and gloves

Footwear is a personal matter, but it should be slip-proof and should keep your feet dry. Some people prefer wellingtons (although these are not welcomed by skippers because of the skid-marks they can leave on the deck), while others feel comfortable in trainers or old leather shoes that are past polishing.

Leather or wool gloves protect, prevent slipping and in cold weather, enable your hands to function.

The nonslip leather footwear worn by yachtsmen is ideal, either with socks or without.

Always have protective gloves; handling a shark with bare hands will leave them sore for a long time. Watch the skipper and see when he first puts on thick leather gloves. On your own boat, where you are the skipper, you must have heavy-duty gloves available. Sore, lacerated hands and fishing gear do not go together.

When you board the boat, make sure all ID material, car keys, wallet and so on are secure in a zipped-up inside pocket or stowed away securely below or in a covered hatch. An unlocked tackle box is not the place. A large charterboat may have a safe or lockable cupboard for valuables.

LIFE JACKETS, BELTS AND FLOTATION SUITS

Falling overboard is always a possibility, even in calm seas, and all sea-going boats must carry sufficient gear to ensure the safety of everyone on board.

Life jackets that are worn around the neck are more comfortable than the old-fashioned life belts and do a better job of keeping your head above water. In many countries they are mandatory safety items without which no boat may leave port.

A flotation suit is a buoyant, boiler-suit-like garment that assists you to float and helps keep you warm in the sea.

All safety equipment must be easily accessible, not locked away in a cupboard and must be properly maintained.

HOW TO USE A LIFE JACKET

No angler should go beyond sight of land in a boat that does not carry a minimum of safety equipment such as flares, a radio and lifejackets.

- Place the uninflated life jacket around your neck; run the straps across your back and tie them securely around your waist. Once the life jacket is secure, pull the cord to inflate it.
- Always try to inflate the life jacket before taking to the water.
- An emergency valve allows air to be blown into the life jacket for manual inflation or topping up.
- A whistle incorporated into the jacket serves as a signalling device to guide rescuers towards you. Some models contain a luminous light stick for night rescues.
- Life jackets should be well maintained and regularly inspected.

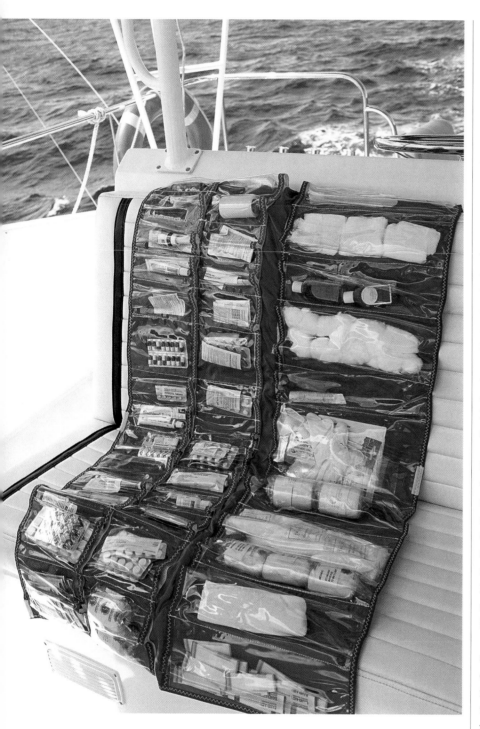

A comprehensive first-aid kit is essential safety equipment for all boats, but anglers should also carry a few basic items in their tackle box.

For the sea angler the most likely calls for first aid will come from bait-knives, hooks or stumbling as the boat rolls and yaws.

Charterboats will always carry first-aid equipment, as they do not want to be accused of not being able to cope with even a slight injury, and at sea there can be a number. But do not expect all boats to have this equipment; you can easily accommodate a few basic items in your tackle carrier.

SUN PROTECTION

One does not have to live in the tropics to become sunburned. In an open boat out at sea, a pleasant breeze can mask the powerful effect of the sun on unprotected skin until too late. The cause of sunburn is ultraviolet radiation, which targets exposed skin. Sunburn is a serious matter and no sensible angler should contemplate going to sea without taking adequate precautions.

A hat with a good-sized brim protects the head; thin sleeves – not open-weave fabric – kept rolled down, will protect the arms. Keep in mind that sunlight reflects off the water, so always apply sunscreen, even if you are wearing a hat and shirt.

There are many prophylactic sun creams and sun blocks available and the first-aid kit should include a waterproof one with a high SP (sun protection) factor, as well as a sun-proof lip-salve. Those who watch cricket matches will have seen the 'white lipstick' used by some team members. It is not war-paint, but zinc-based cream applied to avoid sunburn or, far more importantly, skin cancer. Some sun creams leave permanent stains on fibreglass, which is used extensively on boats. Ask at the shop about this staining before you buy sun cream.

For anglers not used to tropical sunshine, exposure to a hot sun out at sea can lead to heat stroke or heat exhaustion. Heat stroke is the result of body fluids being lost through perspiration and respiration (breath has water droplets in it) and can be alleviated by drinking plenty of water or other cool liquids (but not alcohol), and taking salt tablets.

Heat exhaustion results when the heat-regulation part of the brain ceases to function. This can be serious, and those affected should take salt tablets to help restore the body's chemistry, while the skipper should head for port immediately to obtain medical help back on land.

FIRST AID

Remember that while back on land, emergency help is easy to call up; at sea, with nothing in sight but the horizon, help can take a good deal longer to arrive. Avoiding the need to summon help is a matter of being aware of possible hazards and taking care over all your actions on a sometimes unsteady deck.

FOOD AND DRINK

Although these are not 'treatments', they are equally necessary to maintain stamina and keep the mind and body working properly. Most charterboats will provide plenty of food and liquid refreshments for the duration of the trip, but make sure of this before you board.

Even on a fully-catered charter, many anglers will bring along their favourite snacks or drinks, either as an energy booster or to share with their fellows.

However, be considerate and do not wave food in front of people who are not feeling well.

To avoid dehydration, drink frequently, especially in hot climates. Plain or carbonated water, soft drinks, tea or coffee are preferable to alcohol, which, for safety reasons, is best enjoyed on returning to shore.

SEA SICKNESS

More correctly, this is motion sickness. Fluid normally static in the small channels in the inner ear becomes agitated when a boat is in motion, and this affects the sensory nerves which give rise to motion sickness. Standing and looking at the horizon is said to help, as it concentrates the mind on something not moving up and down, but the only fail-safe cure for sea sickness is to get back onto terra firma.

Sea sickness occasionally takes the form of mass hysteria, with everyone on the boat suddenly looking a bit 'green about the gills'. Taking motion-sickness tablets about half an hour before leaving port should alleviate this affliction though, and every angler should have some in his tackle bag.

There are various types of medication available to treat sea sickness. One, based on scopolamine, the wartime truth drug (but not in the strengths used to drag awkward answers from people!) gives effective relief from *mal-de-mer*, as it is known in in France. Called Transderm-V it is not taken by mouth, but is introduced via a small patch of adhesive material that is applied behind the ear and absorbed into the body. Your physician or pharmacist will be able to advise you on the best method of treatment.

HOOKS

Barbed hooks are designed to prevent the hooked fish from pulling free, but the barbs work just as effectively in human flesh, so do take care when casting, particularly on a crowded boat. Tackle left carelessly lying around on deck can also result in a bare-footed angler inadvertently stepping on a hook.

If a barbed hook does become embedded in flesh, never try to free it by pulling on the eyed end. Either cut through the shank with wire cutters and gently work the embedded barb forward and out through the skin, or, if it is in a dangerous place (near the eye, for instance), cover the wound with a clean dressing and head for home immediately to seek medical help.

FISH TEETH AND SPINES

Many big-game fish, notably the barracuda and wahoo, have strong, powerful teeth, but all fish are able to inflict a nasty wound on a careless angler. A fish that bites the hand that is unhooking it will not only cause the angler some pain, but bacteria from its teeth can be transferred to the wound, giving rise to secondary infection.

Some bottom-feeding species have venomous spines on their gill-covers, and some small sharks have venom-carrying dorsal spines, which will have the same effect. It is wise to wear protective gloves when handling these species. In the event of a scratch or a bite, the first-aid box will be needed and the appropriate antiseptic cream applied.

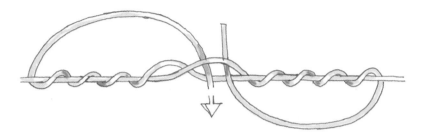

CHAPTER FIVE

TACKLE AND TECHNIQUES

There are many facets to the sport of angling. They cover the freshwater duo of fly fishing and coarse fishing; and the full range of sea fishing modes: beach fishing, rock fishing, pier fishing, inshore boat fishing, and big-game fishing.

The basic equipment for all these branches of the sport is by simple description the same – one needs a rod, a reel, a hook and a bait. In practice this simplicity cannot work, for a slender fly-rod, fly line and small artificial dry fly would be totally useless at sea. So the basic ingredients of fishing – while remaining rods, reels, lines, hooks and baits – change in strength and complexity with each kind of fishing.

TACKLE

Rods and reels cannot do the job without the associated accessories: rings, reels and reel seatings, swivels and links, weights, line and hooks.

There are other accessories without which the angler should not put to sea, such as bait boards, gaffs (to be used only when absolutely necessary), bait knives, pliers for extracting hooks from tough jaws and protective gloves, as well as appropriate clothing and sustenance, as discussed.

Salt water is a highly corrosive substance and through oxidization will quickly reduce to rust things made of iron. Tackle manufacturers do their best to combat this by using suitable metallic compounds which go some way to combating oxidization in reels, rod rings, hooks, swivels and other tackle. Nevertheless, all tackle used in sea fishing should be washed thoroughly in fresh water as soon as possible on reaching base.

Lever drag multiplier reels are an essential factor in big-game fishing tackle.

Deep-sea fish species are almost all powerful predatory creatures and the strength that they use in chasing and subduing their prey-fish is turned to good account when they take the baited hook. In a simple man-to-fish contest a large big-game fish would win every time. It is a combination of the angler's experience and skill, as well as his choice of tackle, with its strength, pliability, dependability all in unison, which allows him to hook, play and eventually bring the fish to the boat.

RODS

Even when at anchor, sea anglers have to contend with the pull of the tide, the motion of the boat, the necessity to reel in a fish that may have been hooked deep down on the seabed, to say nothing of the strength of many species of sea fish. Strength and reliability coupled with lightness are the basic requirements of all fishing rods, but big-game rods must be able to take more punishment than most.

Not that long ago boat-fishing rods were sturdy, heavy things. Some were made of split or whole cane, many of solid wood (hickory and greenheart were two of the woods used) and some were of bamboo and as thick as a cavalry lance. The accepted attitude was that, since sea fishing demanded power from the angler and strength from the rod, there was no necessity for subtlety.

After World War II there was a universal desire for relaxation and anglers soon renewed their love of the sport. New tackle was needed and an unusual source of fishing rods was found: the aerials from thousands of unwanted armoured vehicles. The aerials were fairly light, had the pliability needed in fishing rods, and with butt-end and rings attached, they found a considerable market.

Tubular steel was another experiment, claiming lightness, but it had a tendency to collapse in mid-section, and inner rusting soon brought an end to the use of these rods.

The next step forward was the introduction of solid fibreglass in the postwar era. This material allowed for rods (known cynically by freshwater anglers as 'billiard cues') that were strong and fairly light by the standards of the time.

Hollowglass followed in the 1960s. Made from a fibre moulded round a cylindrical mandrel, cut into sections and fitted with rings and a butt-end, this allowed for a still lighter rod. Unfortunately, like tubular metal, this material also had the tendency to fold or fracture under pressure.

It was around this time that rods made from aluminium came on the market. These allowed for a saving in weight, but the metal fishing rods did not last long, for other materials were being developed. Technology soon produced tubular fibre, or graphite, followed by Kevlar and boron, which produced amazingly light, immensely strong rods, ideally suited for their purpose.

A line-up of big-game fishing rods stand ready for action. Note the two rods mounted higher for trolling. When a fish strikes, the active rod is removed to allow the angler free movement.

Today, as technology continues to advance, rod manufacture has become a hi-tech business, with a number of well-known, international brands offering a range of rods for all types of sea angling.

In order to cope with the brute strength of the really big-game fish species without exhausting the angler, rods are designed in IGFA 24kg (50 lb), 37kg (80 lb) and 60kg (130 lb) classes, with line-breaking strains to match. In determining records, line class is the deciding factor, as the line, which is the connecting link between fish and man, can fail no matter how powerful the rod.

The record lists in the annual IGFA handbook reflect the rod classes by listing records caught in each one. However there does need to be provision for the heaviest catch of any species, no matter what tackle is used, so there is another list for all-tackle records – the heaviest fish caught by an angler using any line-class up to 60kg (130 lb). This does give a fairer indication of the difference between hooking and boating a really big, possibly record, fish and a medium-sized specimen on the same rod and line, for the angling achievement is different: there can be no satisfaction in easily reeling in a fish on gear that is far too powerful.

There are many variables in rod design, depending on usage. Most rods used at sea measure between 1.8–2.4m (6–8ft) in length, although trolling rods are shorter than this. For record purposes, the IGFA equipment regulations demand that the rod-tip must be a minimum of 1m (40in) long and the butt a maximum of 0.68m (27in). Curved butts, developed for use in the fighting chair and known in some areas as 'banana butts', are measured as a straight line.

A growing number of anglers who do not wish to be constricted by the fighting chair, have rods designed specifically for them. These are considerably shorter than the traditional big-game rods, measuring between 1.5–1.8m (5–6ft), and have a shorter butt-end than usual, as well as a fast taper to give lots of action.

Ultimately, each angler must select the best rod for the conditions he is fishing under. In all instances, the emphasis should be on strength and reliability. The rod should have a comfortable grip and hold the reel securely, without the slightest suggestion of movement under the strain of the fight.

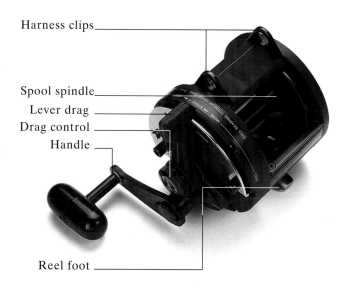

Harness clips

Spool spindle

Lever drag

Drag control

Handle

Reel foot

Roller line guides (above) *and rings* (below) *ensure that the line flows smoothly from reel to rod-tip.*

Rings or line guides

In some kinds of fishing the rings, which are set at carefully calculated distances along the rod to give the maximum test-curve and allow the spring in the rod to work to the angler's advantage, do little more than guide the line from the reel to the rod-tip and then out. A rod's test curve is determined by clamping the rod in a horizontal position and hanging a weight from the rod-tip. The weight needed, given in kilograms or pounds, to bring the rod-tip down to the vertical is the test curve figure. Whether or not the test curve has any value in describing rods manufactured from hi-tech manmade substances such as Kevlar is a moot point, and has been debated since the term was introduced.

On light freshwater rods, the rings are simple circular metal guides, sometimes of stainless steel lined with agate or some other polished lining, and with little to do except keep the wet nylon from clinging to the rod shaft. Big-game fish, however, can put extremely fierce tension on a line, and the pull on the rings, especially near the tip, is often violent, no matter how much the angler tries to keep things nicely under control. This is where roller rings of tungsten carbide, silicon carbide or titanium help, for they keep cool and avoid heat from friction building up as the line moves through them.

REELS

Modern sea-fishing reels are a far cry from the old, huge-diameter, wooden centrepins such as the Scarborough type which had a 1:1 ratio (where one turn of the spool equals one turn of the handle).

The extreme size of the spool diameter was necessary in those days because of the amount of line needed – over 90m (100 yd) of thick monofilament – and before that, yarn or cuttyhunk (a form of flax). Today the centre-pin reel is no longer used for anything but the lightest kind of inshore sea fishing.

1. The Policansky 2020 is an excellent boat reel for tuna. The lever drag allows the drag tension to be gradually and precisely increased.

2. The famous Penn Senator 114HL, with star-drag mechanism, has been the mainstay of medium tackle game fishing around the world for many years.

3. The Shimano TLD20 with lever-drag is an excellent medium to light tackle big-game fish reel with a silky-smooth drag.

4. Although relatively small, the Abu Garcia 6600CL Ambassadeur with star-drag is highly regarded by top big-game anglers.

Multiplier reels

No big-game angler should go to sea without the multiplier-type reel, which is always situated on top of the rod. In fact, the slipping clutch of the multiplier made possible the sport of big-game fishing. As the name suggests, a multiplier has a spool which revolves four or five times for one turn of the handle.

This is possibly the most expensive item of fishing tackle that the angler will have to buy, for it is a precision instrument that enables him to control his rate of retrieve, slow the fish down, and recover line evenly on to the spool without its collapsing under the considerable pressure of hundreds of metres of tightly wound nylon. Added to the cost of the reel will be the line most suited to the fish species being aimed for and the prevailing fishing conditions.

Blue-marlin fishing, for instance, usually requires 24 or 37kg (50 or 80 lb) breaking strain (b.s.) line, while the really big tunas demand 60kg (130 lb) b.s.

Not long ago the American-made Penn Senator reels were used almost exclusively in big-game fishing. This company marketed a range of reels which had a star-drag mechanism, controlled – as the name implies – by a star-shaped wheel which tightened or loosened the revolving ability of the spool independently of the handle, thus putting pressure on a fish other than that of the rod and line alone. One of the problems with the star drag was the generation of friction-based heat, and water had to be sprinkled over the reel whenever steam appeared.

Companies like Abu, Shimano, Diawa and others now manufacture reels with a lever drag, operated

The Scarborough, or centre-pin reel, used for saltwater spinning and boat fishing, has a wide diameter and a 1:1 ratio – where one turn of the handle equals one turn of the spool. The larger version, on the left, can be used for bottom fishing in deep water, where no casting is involved and the hook is set by winding the fish on rather than by striking.

(while the spool is left free-running) by being eased backwards or forwards to increase or reduce the effect of line being pulled off the spool by a still very active fish. The sometimes considerable heat from friction is dissipated by graphite plates, rather like the disc brakes on a car. A level-wind mechanism distributes the line evenly onto the spool during the retrieve and thus avoids potential disaster if the line piles up in one place and clogs the spool or compresses it into a fracture. Reels with lever drag are much more expensive than models with star drag.

Balance between reel and rod is important; the weight should be distributed between them so that when the rod is held lightly the weight of the reel does not pull the rod-tip down, or vice versa if the rod is too heavy. (This does not apply when a fighting chair, harness and rod-holder are in use.)

At the end of every fishing session, do a little maintenance on your reels by washing them in fresh water while the drag is tightened, then loosening it and spraying the moving parts with a thin oil or lubricant. When putting your gear away at the end of the season, take the trouble to wind all the line off your reels onto spare spools to remove any twist that has accumulated. Store your dry, clean reels in cloth or leather bags, or individual waterproof zip-up bags, to avoid damage from dust, rust and so on.

Fixed-spool reels

These are used primarily in freshwater fishing, but there are large sea angling models. Unlike the multiplier reel, where the spool, which is at right angles to the rod, revolves as the handle is turned; the spool of the fixed-spool reel remains motionless while a device called the bale-arm revolves and winds retrieved line onto the spool.

Saltwater spinning, as with freshwater spinning, is done with a fixed-spool reel because of the ease of casting and much better control of line retrieval. The stresses put on sea-angling tackle mean that the fixed-spool reel must be larger and more robust than freshwater models

Maintenance of sea-spinning reels must be even more thorough than that given to freshwater reels. To avoid corrosion, the spool must be taken off after each use and given a good wash in fresh water. Grease or lubricant must be applied to the gearing mechanism before the plate is screwed back on, and a coating of thin oil will help keep down wear.

Electric reels

To the purist, the use of an electric reel may seem like laziness, if not cheating! This is not quite the same as the form of terminal rig which strikes automatically when a fish takes the bait, but it is close. Electric reels are used in freshwater game-fishing and it was inevitable that big-game reels would follow the trend, despite the high costs involved.

An electric reel saves the angler the task of turning the handle to reel the fish in. One tackle manufacturer offers a range of electric power units that can be attached to 16 models in the Penn stable of deep-sea reels. Although there are claims that an electric reel would enable an angler to retrieve a large fighting big-game fish from a depth of up to 640m (2100ft) without him touching the handle, few big-game anglers are ever likely to hook a fish at such depths.

Above *An electric reel may do most of the hard work, but most sportfishermen feel that it removes some of the challenge that attracts them to big-game fishing in the first place.*
Left *This Penn International 50T Wide multiplier reel is set for trolling. A safety line attaches it to the rod.*

LINES

Early fishing lines were made from dyed horsehair, which was plaited and tied to the rod-tip. Attached to this were all kinds of yarn, including linen, silk and cuttyhunk.

The first manmade lines, developed in the 1930s and used in huge quantities for parachute manufacture during World War II, were made from nylon, a compound of '(vy)nyl+(ray)on'. Anglers continued using coarser lines for sea fishing as the thin nylon lines were prone to stretch considerably over the distance from rod to seabed when tide and hooked fish jointly were pulling on them. Nylon is said to weaken when exposed to sunlight, but the author has not experienced this, even when using a reel loaded with nylon after a year's rest.

Monofilament

Soon however, nylon lines, called monofilament ('one filament'), were being manufactured in stronger breaking strains suitable for deep sea fishing, and they have served perfectly well ever since.

In one way, nylon has the disadvantage of stretch (up to about 30 percent before breaking, a factor which can prevent the hook setting); and added to this is the pressure build-up on the spool, mentioned in the previous section, although this is not so important in big-game reels constructed for strength. On the other hand, nylon's ability to stretch could be a saving grace should a potentially disastrous strain suddenly be put on the line by a powerful fish.

Without some ability to stretch, either the line itself would snap or some other element in the tackle would fail and the fish would be lost. The stretch factor was virtually eliminated, however, once synthetic polyester fibre lines came on the market; and this type of line is now used almost exclusively for big-game fishing.

Monofilament is based on compromise, but in general it is reliable and long-wearing with the ability to withstand abrasions and nicks. Polyester fibre lines sold under the trade names Dacron or Terylene have braided versions and are IGFA rated. As they have less stretch than nylon monofilament they can be used for trolling. Braided lines can be unpopular with charterboat skippers because snagging is more likely with a half-dozen lines close together, and a hook-barb lodged in a braided line makes it impossible to clear the reel lines until both lines are retrieved (amid much annoyance).

For record claims, there are rules concerning line usage and, with the exception of all-tackle claims, line classes are limited for many species of fish. The IGFA keeps records for fish taken in the line classes shown in the panel left.

A selection of deep-sea monofilaments and leader material.

Wire line

Wire line, either single-strand or braided, is fine in the right hands and under the right conditions but these lines, for which the rod should be fitted with tungsten-carbide rings or guides, must be kept taut and straight and wound back properly onto the spool. If they are allowed to become loose, the built-in spring created while on the spool will cause total chaos as the wire kinks and clogs, bringing the spool to a permanent stop. Kinks cannot be removed from wire line.

A single-strand wire line has a denoted breaking strain; but when braided it gains strength by the multiplication of single-strand breaking strains.

The line is the direct link between fish and angler, and with wire's increased sensitivity the slightest touch is transmitted back up the line immediately. Other advantages of wire line are that there is no stretch; that in terms of diameter, wire is stronger than monofilament; and that wire line is not so affected by tidal push because of its fine diameter. Wire is also great trolling line. So what are the disadvantages?

There are a few, but the main one is that a kink in wire line is a kink for ever – it cannot be straightened without weakening the wire. Another is that direct tension from hook to angler must be maintained from cast to retrieve. On the spool, wire tends to build up into coils that will become apparent if the line is allowed to go slack, and the retrieve can end in the chaos described above, with the wire clogging up the spool and bringing it to a stop. The tip-ring and intermediates must be of tungsten-carbide, in tip-top condition and able to take wire running through them without damage from friction generated heat. Wire lines do not rust and the only care they require is to be kept free from kinks.

Traces

Angling for any big fish with sharp teeth demands a very strong trace leading down to the hook. It has been suggested that up to 6m (20ft) of 98kg (200 lb) breaking-strain wire is the right length trace for those shark species that roll themselves up in the trace when they detect the hook. These strengths are somewhat high, but whatever trace is selected, swivels must be added to counteract the twisting of the reel line by a fish.

Leaders

When a large fish puts up a terrific struggle, and the pull from the fish is stronger than the line, the rod may suddenly straighten out and the line go slack because it has broken under the strain. Had you added a leader, the line would have parted where the leader and the reel line met, avoiding the loss of

A leader line with two hooks attached using a trace and swivel. This rig has been prepared especially to hold fresh squid to fish for broadbill swordfish.

a long stretch of reel line and possibly preventing damage to the rod itself. The leader line should have a heavier breaking strain than the reel line, and should be strong enough to withstand the biting action of a fish's teeth.

The leader is the link between the reel line and whatever terminal tackle is being used. Unlike in freshwater fishing, where the line's visibility must be kept to a minimum, leaders in saltwater fishing are employed primarily for strength. In the case of predatory big-game saltwater fish, which have teeth designed to cut and rip, delicate tackle presentation is not necessary and leaders can be visible.

Strong piano wire or braided wire is often used. This is attached to the swivels (for which a crimping tool and metal sleeves are necessary). Ready-made Sampo swivel leaders are available with test strains from 15cm/10kg (6in/20 lb) to 90cm/20kg (3ft/45 lb).

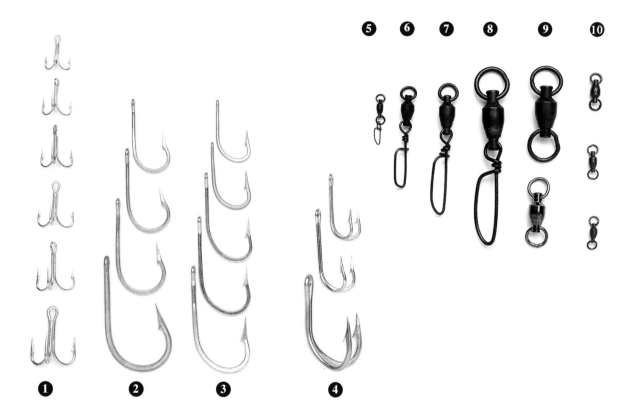

HOOKS

The hook is the angler's first contact with the fish and the last line of resistance as it comes to the boat. The purchase of top-quality hooks is to be recommended and brands such as Mustad, Partridge, Wright & McGill, Kamasan and Redditch, have been in the business since the early 19th century. With the trade names come the famous models, patterns and bends, such as O'Shaughnessy, Aberdeen, Kirby, Limerick and Viking, all of which serve some particular angling style.

Every part of a hook, from shank, bend and throat to barb, point and eye, may vary. Mustad, possibly the biggest name in fishing hooks, has some 60,000 patterns on offer.

For the purposes of big-game fishing, the top sizes of hooks come into use, and run from size 9/0, through 10/0, 12/0, 13/0, 14/0, 15/0 to 16/0. The last size might appear to resemble a small anchor sitting in the tacklebox, but when compared with the size of a large shark's jaws it pales into insignificance!

Sharpness can be tested with a cautious thumb. Barbs should not be cut too deeply otherwise the point will break away at the moment of take.

The eye must be smooth so that it will not wear away the line, and its temper must be right or the eye will straighten under tension.

At the end of every trip out, sea anglers should dip all their tackle into a bucket of fresh water, as sea water is very corrosive and hooks, especially, suffer from quick rusting unless they are stainless steel (stainless steel and carbon steel hooks need nothing more than a wipe-over with an oiled cloth.

Excessive wear can, however, affect hook coatings and given the chance the salt water will start its destructive work, so even if they are of stainless steel, dry hooks should always be kept in sealable plastic bags.

SWIVELS

There are some fish species that make violent twisting movements (as sharks do when feeding to tear away flesh), and this can spoil things at the last moment. Any swivel must, therefore, do just that, for its purpose is to prevent line and terminal tackle from twisting to destruction.

There is no substitute for top-class swivels, and the internationally-renowned, US-made Berkley and

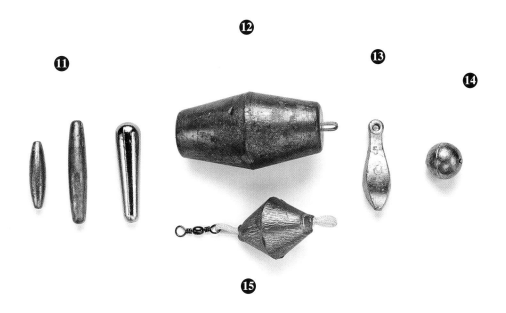

HOOKS, SWIVELS AND WEIGHTS

Shown smaller than actual size, is a selection of tackle suitable for sea angling.

1 Treble hooks are fitted to lures, plugs and spinners used for tuna fishing. The strengthened variety are recommended.

2 For very powerful fish, forged steel hooks with straight round eyes are preferable, as they allow the hook to move on the trace. They are obtainable up to size 16/0.

3 These hooks have been formed with the Limerick bend, the distinctive shape bend being an asset when large artificial flies are to be used as lures for spinning and fly-fishing at sea.

4 Double hooks are used mostly by commercial tuna fishermen.

5-8 Link swivels, ranging from 13–127kg (30–280 lb) pull, are used for clipping on traces and leader lines. There are three variations, the snap-link, buckle-link and diamond eye. Three-way swivels (not shown) can also be used to attach a leader off the main line, for swimming an alternative bait among the main one.

9-10 Ball-bearing swivels are extremely smooth and give the best protection against line twist and kink when trolling.

11 Three laterally-pierced barrel sinkers, used on sliding rigs to hold the bait at the required depth.

12 This heavy broadbill weight holds the bait at the required depth when drifting in a strong current.

13 The bottle sinker is used mainly for rock and surf fishing.

14 A ball sinker is used for light tackle boat fishing when drift is desirable.

15 The boat and cord sinker is used mainly by commercial handline fishermen.

Sampo and Mustad ranges stand out in this respect. Wherever you are, the rule is to buy the best available.

Ball-bearing swivels from sizes 1 to 8 are reputed to be the strongest available and they come in ratings to 227kg (500 lb). Link and snap models, also with ball-bearings, are manufactured to 136kg (300 lb) rating. For the heaviest fish, there are swivels rated at 159kg (350 lb) test, and considering that they may have to bear the weight of a big marlin, they must be reliable. Different swivels should be kept in separate plastic envelopes in your tackle box.

WEIGHTS

Big-game anglers rarely fish in waters where the seabed can be reached. On the few occasions when they do, however, weights (or sinkers) are used.

Forget about weights that are measured in grams or ounces. The power in a tide will lift anything under 1kg (2 lb) off the seabed and the line itself offers considerable resistance over its length. Weights can be pear-shaped, circular, have studs that grip the bottom, or have projecting wires that grip the seabed.

GAFFS AND TAILERS

A gaff is a large piece of forged steel with a very sharp, barbless hook screwed into its head. The rule today is to use the gaff only when absolutely necessary, and only if you intend to kill the fish (if possible, return your catch alive to the water.)

Since it is designed to enter flesh and stay there, the pointed barb of a gaff will do the job just as efficiently in the human body. Do not leave the gaff head unprotected, cover it with a short length of plastic tubing.

In the right hands and at the right time, the use of a gaff is acceptable – fish weighing up to about 11kg (25 lb) can usually (depending on the species) be lifted inboard and killed quickly by a hard, sharp blow on the head. However, a large, strong, thrashing specimen, such as a shark or a billfish, very often cannot be pulled over the side. In this

SHOCK LEADERS FOR CASTING

Some big-game fishing is deliberately carried out with light tackle in order to improve the quality of the sport when casting. In this case, a shock leader of 27kg (60 lb) line is attached to the end of the reel line to take the strain and shock of casting 170g (6oz) weights while fishing with 6.8kg (15 lb) line. As the weight of the lead increases, the shock leader's breaking strain will rise accordingly.

TACKLE BOX

Tackle boxes come in as many different variants as there are anglers, but any tackle box should be of stout plastic (wood soon rots in a wet atmosphere) and should be watertight. The most commonly used modern tackle box resembles an engineer's metal or plastic tool box, opening concertina-like and displaying layers of shelves. Each shelf is composed of compartments in which the angler keeps his many accessories: different types of swivels, hooks of various sizes, leaders, lures, jigs, plugs, a hook sharpener, spare spools of line of different breaking strains and much else, depending upon the size of the box.

Above (top to bottom) *Flying gaff, a selection of gaffs for various weights of fish, and a landing net, which is useful for smaller specimens and bait fish.*

situation, the flying gaff is better – when the hook goes home, the gaff head pulls away from the pole but is held by a chain attached to the boat, and the fish remains in the water until, usually, a second gaff or tailer is used to immobilize the fish. A tailer is a running loop, often of wire, which is put over the tail of a big fish, and pulled tight and upwards to get the tail out of the water.

Above *Lures attached to the leader line lie ready for action.*
Right *Every angler will keep his tackle box stocked with his favourite lures, spinners, plugs and accessories.*

Keep your tackle box well secured, under a seat if possible. Tripping over it and spilling the contents will lose you friends and extend your vocabulary!

Always keep the box closed and try to keep it away from any sea spray. Sea water that has found its way into your box will begin to attack any metal that can be oxidized.

SCALES

It has been said that the biggest fish any angler has ever caught was the one he unhooked and released. Weighing scales, which come in various models (but for recording purposes must be accurate), are useful for weighing fish that are to be released at sea.

For official record purposes, weighing a fish on board and releasing it is not acceptable to the IGFA. The fish must be brought ashore, properly identified and weighed on scales that are regularly checked by an official and certified as accurate.

TECHNIQUES

In freshwater fishing much is made of the technique of 'reading the water' – assessing the effects of wind, the flow of the stream, the light conditions and the depth. At sea, some of these conditions also apply, such as swirls on the surface, small fish leaping and scattering or seabirds diving or hovering over one area. Fish feeding on the surface create eddies and swirls as they turn and strike; the human eye can easily spot the dorsal fin of a shark or the tailfin of a marlin as it

Left Hand-held scales are essential for weighing fish that are to be tagged and released. Below A crimping tool firmly attaches leaders to lines. Bottom The shock leader helps take the strain of casting.

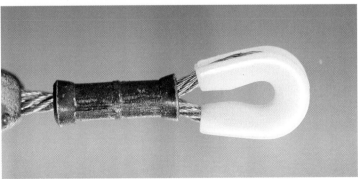

cuts the waves. Ex-US Navy man Al Ristori has written about how he picks up the scent of a feeding tuna or bluefish by the 'watermelon' smell of the slick the fish leaves in the water. All these signs should be noted, for they tell of the presence of fish and they can be acted upon.

In angling lore, much is made of the angler's 'sixth sense'. When nothing has been happening for some time, when all the rod-tops are still and the lines running out and showing no movement (which has been described as 'like waiting for paint to dry'), an angler may suddenly sense action. And sure enough, the rod-tip will begin to quiver, the line running from the top ring will straighten or the snap holding the line to the outrigger will give an electrifying twitch. Whether this sixth sense is real or not, this is the moment when techniques come into play.

One sense that retains much of its primitiveness is that of touch – the nerve endings in the fingers are extremely sensitive to the slightest twitch or shudder. This is one reason to hold the rod for as long as possible, with a finger resting on the line above the reel. With experience (and a tight line), you will learn to detect the first nudge of a fish 90m (100 yd) away, and be ready to act when the bite comes.

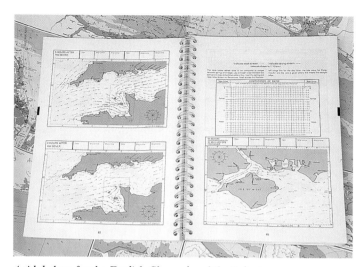

A tidal chart for the English Channel and the Solent.

TIDES

Sea anglers need to know how the tides affect the movements of the sea and the fish themselves. Tide charts are often available from fishing-tackle shops.

Tide times are fixed in Tahiti, where the moon's influence is minimal, so the tide is high at midnight and midday and low as the sun goes down and again when it rises. At various places round the earth, however, tides are strikingly different. In the English Channel, between the Isle of Wight and the mainland, for instance, there are four tides a day, while the Mediterranean Sea has virtually no tides at all. In global terms, tides are smaller in rise and fall near the equator, increasing towards the poles.

The words spring and neap are applied to tides: spring has nothing to do with the season, but refers to a rise in the water level, while neap refers to tides which have very little effect on water movement. Spring tides occur when the sun and moon act together, their combined gravitational pull creating high tides; when the sun and moon do not act in unison the tides are weak.

The height of the tide in any place depends on the local topography of the seabed and can vary a great deal, from 0.6–0.9m (2–3ft) to more than 2.4m (8ft). In some places the tide rises and falls as much as 6–9m (20–30ft). In deep water, the habits of surface-feeding fish species are not affected by tidal movement as much as inshore species living in and around rocks and sandy bays, but even out fairly deep some species do react to tides more than others. In general, fish stop feeding as the tide slackens and resume when the sea begins to flow again.

TROLLING

This classic fishing style goes back to the Polynesians, from whom 19th-century visiting anglers copied it after realizing its usefulness.

Trolling enables the angler to cover a wide area of sea, and it presents a bait on a hook in a lifelike manner. The baits used will depend on the location and species sought – usually marlin, wahoo, sailfish, bonito and tuna. Black marlin are particularly susceptible to trolled fish of about 3kg (6–7 lb). Trolled baits can be live or dead food-fish, or one of the many lures on the market (*see* Baits, page 54).

The movement of the trolled fish-bait through the water must be as realistic as possible, and this will

not happen if the hook is simply stuck through the fish's lower jaw before the bait is let out.

To prepare a bait for trolling, slit the fish from the anal orifice to close to the gill covers, then remove the backbone. Insert the hook through the mouth, allowing the barb (not the shank) to project. An extra refinement is to sew the mouth closed, as this allows the bait to 'swim' more cleanly and, without the stiffening of the backbone, the fish's body will wriggle attractively as it is trolled.

When towing a line behind a moving boat there is always the possibility of the line becoming twisted. If the swivels are working properly, they can eliminate line twist, and there are plastic swivel-covers with vanes which also help. Without swivels however, the line is sure to twist unless the bait is mounted so that it does not spin.

If the bait needs to be towed below the surface, a sinker can be attached, and the speed of the boat and weight of the sinker can be adjusted so that the bait moves at the required depth. Big-eye tuna, wahoo and bluefish can all be caught by trolling at depths of down to 30m (100ft).

The depth at which the bait is trolled is decided by a combination of speed and weight, but bear in mind that the weight of the bait in the hand bears little resemblance to its weight in water, and allowance must be made for this. As a boat's speed falls, the weighted terminal tackle will sink lower.

Much depends on the speed of the boat (usually about 3–4 knots, with a maximum of 7–8 knots), as any deviation between the normal speed of the food-fish when it's alive and when it is being trolled may decide the matter. Sharks, for instance, seem not to

Rods fixed for trolling from a moving boat. When a strike occurs, they can quickly be removed from the holders and clipped into the rod butt or harness.

want to work up any speed to chase a bait being trolled at 'marlin' speed; so when the telltale shark dorsal fin cuts the water towards the bait, the wise skipper will reduce the speed of the boat.

The set of the reel, with the drum free, is an important factor in trolling. The drag must be set so that the lure's action through the water is insufficient to pull line off the spool. This anticipates a sudden powerful lunge from a fish, for if the drum is locked when the fish strikes, something could break.

On a boat carrying four anglers, the best way to troll is by staggering the baits on lines of varying length, with two of the lines on outriggers.

SPINNING

Spinning, in big-game fishing terms, has little to do with the time-honoured art of spinning in fresh water, yet even at sea, spinning is a busy, active method of fishing.

There is one important similarity between freshwater and saltwater spinning, and that is the reel, which must be a large fixed-spool model. Spinning with any other kind of reel (such as a multiplier or centre-pin) is very difficult. Fixed-spool reels for saltwater spinning are attached below the rod and

Anglers off Cape Town, South Africa, use spinning and drifting techniques to catch yellowtail and yellowfin tuna.

are much larger than freshwater reels. The rods, in about the 1.8kg (6 lb) class, are designed specifically to accommodate the reel and have plenty of action.

The technique is to cast the lure (a plug, spinner or spoon) to wherever you think the fish are (casting distance is made easier by the fixed-spool reel), allow the lure to reach the depth required, then reel it back. The speed of retrieval depends on many factors, including the size and weight of lure, the depth at which the angler wants the lure to swim, the colour of the water and the species being fished.

With practice, very fish-like movements can be given to a lure, suggesting a scurrying through the water or a rise- and-fall action as if by a wounded fish. Plugs such as the Rapala with a vane fitted will rise as you retrieve the line and sink when you stop.

DRIFTING

This can be carried out either with the engine shut down, or idling slowly enough to just nudge the boat along. With the engine off, there are no vibrations through the propellor which might be detected by fish and scare them away.

The most important element in drift fishing is the speed of the boat in relation to the tide. Between tides or when there is no wind, there will be little or no drift, while wind and tide moving in the same direction can create a too-fast drift. In these circumstances, the drogue or wind-anchor (*see* page 69) can slow you down.

Moving with the current, suspended baits will be in a natural position and feeding fish are likely to accept one. The drift rig is suspended at the required depth by a float or a balloon which is attached by a sliding peg which pulls the line free as the fish dives. When you use a suspended bait, much depends upon the seabed over which the boat is drifting. The use of an echo-sounder helps to ensure that baits are suspended in the best position.

Large sharks can be taken on the drift, using whole bait such as mackerel, bonito or whatever food-fish are in the area. Broadbill swordfish are also taken by commercial fishermen who work on the drift at night, the darkness and lack of engine noise being good cover for the notoriously wary swordfish, which has high commercial value. Big-game anglers in some parts of the world copy this technique with some success.

FLY-FISHING

This is an exciting form of blue-water fishing but the rod, reel, line and fly must all be suitable for the type of fish sought, otherwise frustration will overcome the thrill.

The IGFA lists fly-fishing records for big-game fish, with marlin, tuna and even shark, including a blue shark of 83.46kg (184 lb), taken by this method.

The technique of casting a virtually weightless artificial fly demands some skill. To do this the weight of the line is combined with the action of the rod in a series of back-and forth actions until the rod is thrust forward and the line unrolls, allowing the bait to settle gently on the selected patch of water. The same technique is followed for fresh or salt water, but fly-fishing is even more of a sporting exercise at sea, for hooking a strong and weighty fish on a fly rod is not guaranteed to bring it to the boat.

BOTTOM FISHING

As this is done at anchor, it is essential that the boat is in water shallow enough for the purpose. With bottom fishing, the bait is let down to the seabed and held there by a suitable weight. A careful assessment of the strength of the tide must be made to ensure that a taking fish will not feel the resistance of the weight and let the bait go. European waters and the eastern side of the Atlantic are generally suitable for fishing a bait on or close to the seabed, due to the preponderance of large, bottom-feeding fish species, such as common skate and halibut, in these seas.

PLAYING THE FISH

With the smaller species of sea fish, playing them is straightforward: keep the rod up and the line taut, and give line if necessary.

But when that very first big-game fish takes your baited hook, and you have a top-flight rod, expensive reel, the correct breaking-strain line and a fighting chair and harness to hand, there might be a temptation to make this a man-against-fish struggle. Don't! There is more strength in a big blue marlin than you'll ever appreciate, and it is in its natural element. Just keep the pressure on and do not try to bully a large, powerful fish – the chances are you will lose both the fight and the fish.

Line twist on the spool can build up into a potentially dangerous bird's nest, but it can be avoided by

'pumping' the fish, a technique favoured by inshore anglers: with the rod held high, the reel handle is turned and line recovered while pulling the rod down to the horizontal; and the movement is repeated after the rod is again held high.

One way to avoid tangled lines when a number of anglers are fishing from the same boat is to keep a straight line between rod-tip and fish. This is done by moving about the boat, ducking under lines and, sometimes, with the help of a fellow crew member, pointing the rod-tip into the water and passing the rod under the screw or the anchor line (keeping a tight hold on the rod!). Needless to say, if the angler is buckled into a fighting chair, he must be released as quickly as possible.

When a big fish is on the hook and the fight is particularly difficult, and reeling in the monster is putting huge strain on both rod and angler, the skipper must play his part too. Once the fish has stopped circling, as it usually does immediately on taking the bait and feeling resistance, the skipper should keep a careful watch on the angle of the line between rod-tip and surface, which gives an approximation of where the fish is. The skipper must then begin to slowly back the boat towards the fish, which will help the angler to reel the line in, using the pull-up-and-wind-down method. The other anglers or crew members should clear the deck and stand ready with the gaff.

Keeping a straight line between the rod-tip and the fish helps to avoid tangled lines and frayed tempers.

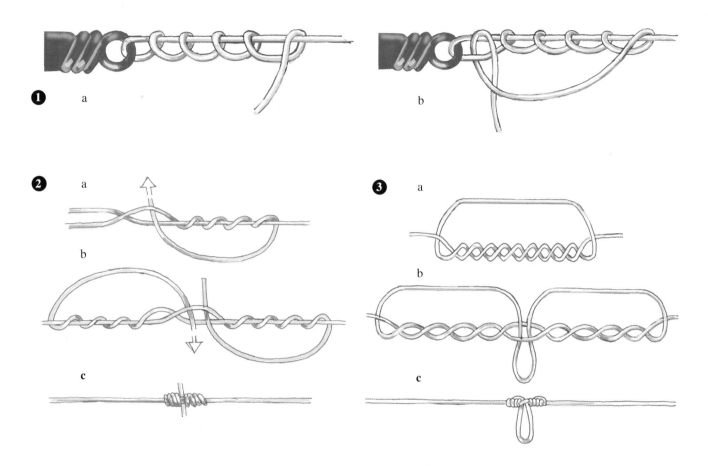

1 a   b

2 a   **3** a

b   b

c   c

BASIC KNOTS

Knots have become an art form in themselves but in truth the big-game angler needs to be familiar with no more than four or six; those for attaching hooks to the line, swivels, leader, plugs, jigs and feathers; those for joining two lengths of monofilament, either of the same or of different diameters; and those for joining monofilament to wire line.

It will come as no surprise to learn that names of knots are just as liable to be affected by local preferences as the names of many fish, but the efficiency of the knot is what is important, not its name.

There are a few basic rules: (a) when tying double lines they must be kept parallel; (b) when putting turns round a standing line, the turns must be kept apart, then tightened neatly; and (c) knots should be tightened under steady, even pressure, ensuring they do not slip (slipping monofilament can create heat, resulting in a weakening of the line). The diagrams above should be quite easy to understand. With practice, even occasional anglers should soon be proficient at tying the basic knots.

HALF-BLOOD KNOT (1)

The knot that attaches the hook to the line is the prime link between the angler and the fish, and if it slips, the fish and hook are gone. The 'half' is therefore probably the first knot an angler learns to tie.

There is a tucked form, in which the end of the line, after passing through the eye of the hook, is taken back to the last loop at the other end.

When either of these two knots is finished, clip off any loose ends to avoid them snagging in rod rings or creating accidental loops in your own or someone else's line.

FULL-BLOOD AND OFFSET-NAIL KNOT (2)

Two flexible strands of material are easy to unite by a knot, but two strands of monofilament are notorious for being difficult to join together as the slightest slippery link will cause the strands pull apart. Any knot in monofilament is the weakest part of the line and decreases its breaking strain by putting pressure on a weak spot.

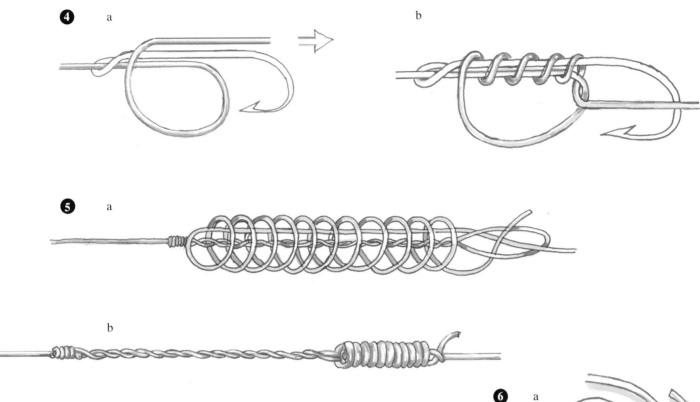

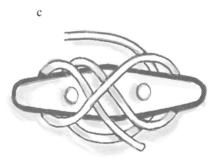

The best knot to use for this job is the full-blood. As the name implies, the full-blood is made from two half-blood knots side by side. Tying a full-blood knot appears very awkward at first, for it seems to need two separate actions, but it is accomplished by taking one side at a time. This knot is effective only when both lengths of monofilament are approximately of the same diameter. If they are not, the offset-nail knot should be used. The name refers to the nail that is used when the knot is being tied, then removed when the ends are pulled tight.

A variation, the surgeon's knot, can also be used when the lines are of different diameters.

BLOOD LOOP (3)

This clever knot produces a loop, or 'snood', in a single strand of monofilament. When a blood loop is formed, the line should be lubricated before the line on either side of the loop is pulled (or eased) firmly together, so that the rings tighten securely.

FRANZ DOMHOF KNOT (4)

This is a variation on the half-blood knot, and is used for the same purpose – to attach monofilament to the eye of a hook. The difference is at the end, when the loose end is taken back and passed under and through the loop.

ALBRIGHT KNOT (5)

This is used when attaching monofilament to wire or leader lines of different diameters, or to attach long leaders to fly line.

BERTHING KNOTS (6)

Although these are not used in fishing as such, any angler worth his salt must be as familiar with the half hitch, clove hitch and cleat hitch as he is with his favourite fishing mark, as these are the knots used to secure the boat to its moorings. An improperly tied berthing knot could result in excessive movement, causing damage to your boat, or the next-door one, and resulting in costly insurance claims.

Wherever big-game fish are to be found there will be anglers seeking to catch them. Some species (see Chapter Two) are prevalent throughout the tropical and subtropical oceans (although not always with the same common names), while others are confined to specific areas.

This branch of sea angling was once very parochial; anglers pursued their favourite species in their part of the ocean, aware that other parts of the world had similar attractions, but rarely having the time or money to travel long distances to fish those areas. Today, with reasonably priced air-tickets and many international airlines to choose from, practically any part of the world is within reach of the dedicated sportfisherman.

The main areas for game fishing (by no means in order of importance), include southern California and the Hawaiian islands in the United States; the Caribbean, including the Bahamas, Costa Rica, Jamaica and the West Indies; the Cape Peninsula at the southern tip of South Africa; Kenya in East Africa; the islands of the Indian Ocean, including the Seychelles, Mauritius and Reunion; the coast of northern Queensland in Australia; the Bay of Islands on New Zealand's North Island; Costa Rica, Panama and Belize in Central America; and the Iberian Peninsula, Balearic Islands, Azores, Canary Islands, Madeira and Gibraltar in Europe.

Most anglers with limited time and money will use the services of a charter company to plan their trip, but those travelling independently to big-game fishing venues with which they are not familiar should never arrive without making every effort to obtain prior knowledge of local fishing regulations, accommodation options, boat availability and costs, species known to frequent the area and, of course, the current state of the fishing.

Write to the local tourist office for the addresses of angling organizations, marinas and charterboat owners, and information about the best fishing seasons, tackle and bait availability.

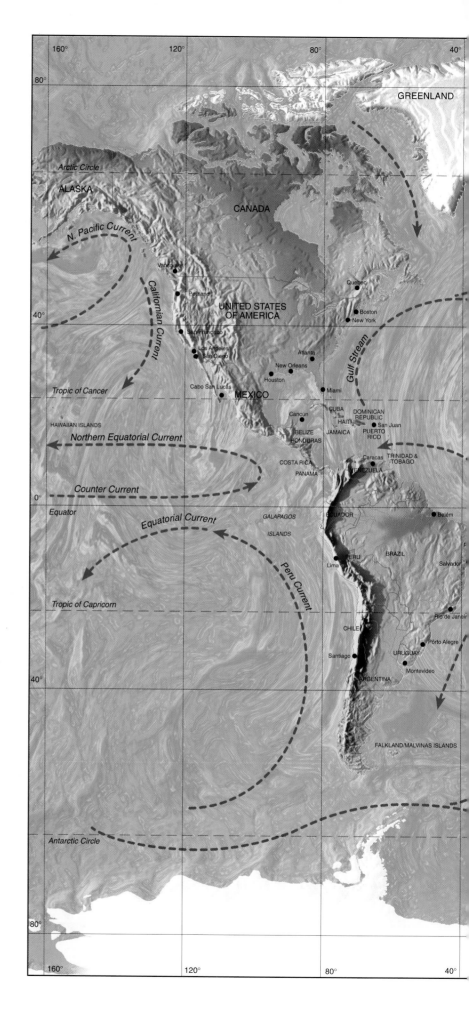

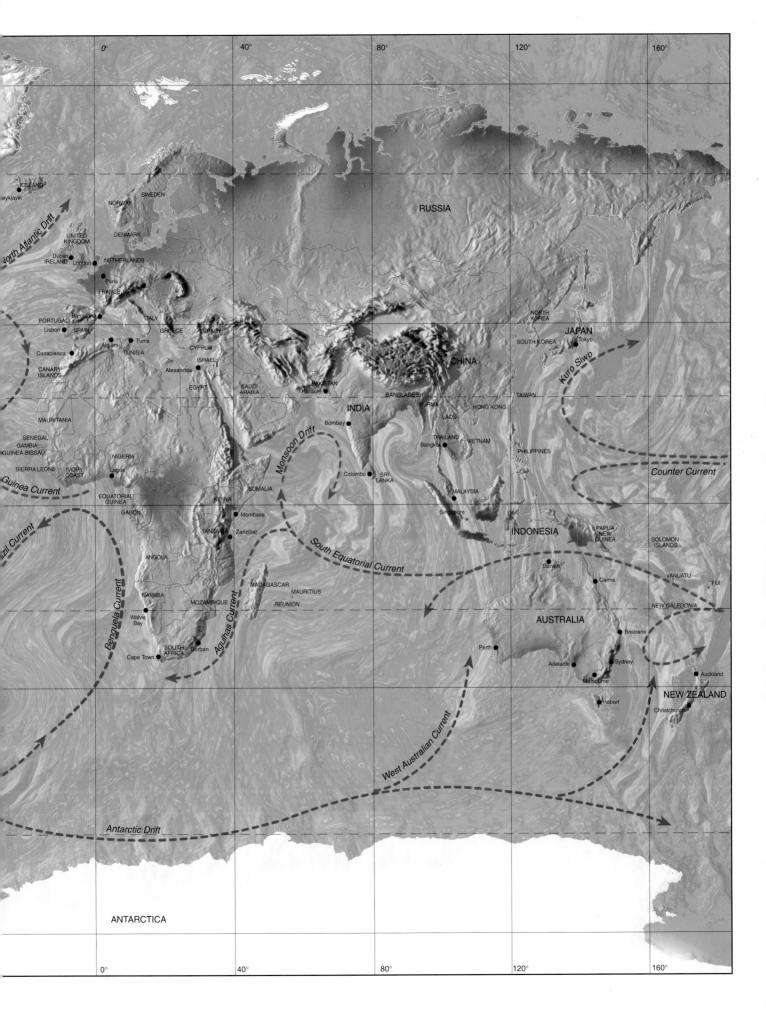

0° 40° 80° 120° 160°

ICELAND
eykjavik

North Atlantic Drift

NORWAY SWEDEN
DENMARK
UNITED
KINGDOM
Dublin
IRELAND London NETHERLANDS
Paris
FRANCE
PORTUGAL Barcelona
Lisbon SPAIN
Casablanca Algiers Tunis
CANARY TUNISIA
ISLANDS

RUSSIA

NORTH
KOREA

SOUTH KOREA JAPAN
Tokyo

Kuro Siwo

ITALY
GREECE TURKEY
CYPRUS
ISRAEL
Alexandria
EGYPT SAUDI
ARABIA Karachi
PAKISTAN

CHINA

TAIWAN

MAURITANIA

SENEGAL
GAMBIA
GUINEA-BISSAU
SIERRA LEONE IVORY
COAST NIGERIA
Lagos
Guinea Current EQUATORIAL
GUINEA KENYA
GABON

INDIA
Bombay

BANGLADESH
BURMA
LAOS
THAILAND VIETNAM
Bangkok

HONG KONG

PHILIPPINES

Colombo SRI
LANKA

Monsoon Drift

SOMALIA

MALAYSIA
Singapore

INDONESIA PAPUA
NEW
GUINEA SOLOMON
ISLANDS

Counter Current

azil Current

ANGOLA

Mombasa
TANZANIA Zanzibar

South Equatorial Current

Darwin

VANUATU

FIJI

Benguela Current

NAMIBIA

Agulhas Current

MADAGASCAR
MAURITIUS
RÉUNION

MOZAMBIQUE

Walvis
Bay

Cape Town Durban
SOUTH
AFRICA

Perth

AUSTRALIA

Cairns

NEW CALEDONIA

Brisbane

Sydney
Adelaide
Melbourne

Auckland

West Australian Current

Hobart

NEW ZEALAND
Christchurch

Antarctic Drift

ANTARCTICA

0° 40° 80° 120° 160°

CHAPTER SIX

THE AMERICAS

Brushed by the temperate Atlantic on the east coast and the warm Pacific on the west, the continents of North and South America offer a wide range of experiences for the dedicated angler.

From the frigid waters of the Canadian Arctic and the subantarctic seas off Chile and Argentina, through to the tropical heat of Mexico and the Caribbean, the angler can choose his destination to suit his recreational preferences as well as his pocket. Big-game anglers, however, will turn naturally towards those countries and regions where they are most likely to catch what they are seeking and the Americas do not disappoint.

Top destinations include Hawaii, which offers possibly the best marlin fishing in the world, both coasts of Mexico, the islands of the Caribbean and the Florida Keys. However, for the determined angler, there are plenty of fishing challenges waiting no matter where he chooses to enjoy his sport.

Sea fishing should be both relaxing and exciting. How anglers react to prevailing weather and sea conditions depends upon their experience and ability to fish at sea in all its various moods. For all but the most dedicated and intrepid angler, the preference is for warm sun and reasonably calm seas, making spring and summer generally the favoured times to go fishing, unless one is lucky enough to be fishing in the tropics.

UNITED STATES OF AMERICA

The cost of charterboat fishing in the USA ranges from moderate to expensive, depending on the size and luxury of the boat and equipment, but the chances of finding big-game species are excellent for the angler who plans his trip thoroughly.

The Gulf of Mexico beckons anglers who seek its warm blue waters for marlin, sailfish and other big-game species.

In general, the deep-sea fisherman will find his every interest catered for, and tackle prices are very reasonable when compared with the rest of the world. Where sea angling is concerned, an area as vast as the United States of America can be only be discussed state by state.

CALIFORNIA

This state has 1609km (1000 miles) of Pacific coast-line and a huge number of species of big-game fish, including swordfish and striped marlin. Many big-game anglers establish their headquarters at San Diego in the south of the state, where they know

they can find good fishing which includes tuna, barracuda and Californian halibut. The coast sees a run of albacore during the summer months, but good timing and local information are necessary.

Northwest of San Diego are San Clemente, Catalina, Santa Barbara and the other islands in the federally owned Channel Islands Monument, which offer some excellent deep-sea fishing. An anti-clockwise current, centred on Catalina Island, results in higher sea temperatures during the summer months, drawing subtropical species such as striped marlin, swordfish, Pacific bonito and yellowtail into the area.

San Diego is the principal port for long-range excursions south to Baja California and the Coronado Islands, for which a Mexican fishing licence is required.

Catch records indicate that southern California is a major centre of big-game fishing in the eastern Pacific ocean, with excellent facilitiesand year-round fishing for many species.

WASHINGTON

The North Pacific Drift current influences coastal temperatures in this northwestern state and summer sea temperatures here are normally several degrees warmer than those slightly further south.

Deep-sea angling is centred largely on salmon fishing. However, albacore migrate into the area during summer and can be caught trolling with lures or live bait.

FLORIDA

To most of the world, Florida is synonymous with big-game fishing. It was here that big-game angling first developed into a skill and an art. Florida's 719km-long (447-mile) peninsula, with the Atlantic on the east and the Gulf of Mexico on the west, is an angler's paradise.

Australian author and billfishing expert Peter Goadby says that Florida 'leads the way in light tackle of all kinds, particularly fly, jigging, bait casting and spinning,' and he calls it the 'university and trendsetter of successful lure fishing'.

The image of the Florida Keys as a centre for billfishing was impressed into 20th-century consciousness through the novels of Ernest Hemingway and

between the Florida Keys and Cuba at a rate of two to four knots, bringing warm water from the Gulf of Mexico and with it, the legendary blue marlin, bluefin tuna and dolphinfish (or *mahi mahi*).

Among the most important angling centres on the Atlantic coast are Fort Lauderdale, Miami and Palm Beach. Key West, Marathon and Islamorada hold sway on the Keys. Other angling centres are Destin and Fort Walton Beach in the Florida Panhandle.

The full list of big-game species caught off the coast of Florida reads like a specimen fish list. In addition to marlin and sailfish, other species for which the area holds records are amberjack, jewfish (308kg; 680 lb) from Fernandina Beach, permit and pompano. A 198kg (436 lb 12oz) warsaw grouper

Below *The Florida Keys are one of the world's top big-game fishing destinations.*

Zane Grey, and the combination of machismo and mystique they engendered continues to draw anglers from around the world to Key West.

The reason for the area's prominence as a big-game fish destination is the Gulf Stream, which flows

was taken from Destin and a record king mackerel, 40.8kg (90 lb), was caught off Key West. Tarpon regularly weigh in at over 45kg (100 lb). The state record for tarpon is 106kg (234 lb). A number of record shark catches have been made in the state:

Opposite *The California coast offers marlin, tuna and barracuda, as well as scenic beauty.*

The crowded marina at San Diego, California, is testament to the popularity of deep-sea angling in the USA.

A dusky shark of 346.5kg (764 lb) came out of the water off Longboat Key; the record spinner shark, at 86.1kg (190 lb), off Flagler Beach; a hammerhead of 449.5kg (991 lb) was boated at Sarasota; and the record lemon shark, weighing 180kg (397 lb), came from Dunedin. Cobia are also a popular near-shore species. Light tackle fishing and saltwater spinning with lures are both prevalent in Florida. Redfish, snook, bonefish and seatrout are all targeted inshore with light tackle. Offshore, the hunt is for sailfish, wahoo, yellowfin and blackfin tuna and marlin.

HAWAII

These volcanic islands rising from the depths of the Pacific offer some of the best billfishing in the world and are considered by anglers everywhere to be the ultimate big-game fishing destination. The Hawaiian islands are in the path of the northeast trade winds and most fishing is done on the sheltered leeward coasts, with spring and summer being the prime months, although excellent opportunities await adventurous anglers willing to try the blustery channels and rough seas of the windward coasts.

Hawaii's blue marlin and tuna grounds are served by an experienced and professional charter industry, with IGFA-approved scales and weigh-masters readily available.

The Kona coast of Hawaii (often referred to as the Big Island) is a day's boat trip south of Honolulu, or just 20 minutes by air. Anglers come from all over the world to these fishing grounds to experience the thrills of big fish and blue water. Hawaii offers deep water within a few hundred metres of the shore, an attractive option for anglers who prefer not to waste valuable fishing time on long journeys offshore.

Many records have come from Kona's 160km-long (100-miles) coast, including several Pacific blue marlin 'granders' – fish weighing over 1000 lb (454.5kg).

The Hawaiian International Billfish Tournament is fished every summer from Kailua Kona. Between Honokohau Harbour, the state's largest charterboat fishing centre, and Keauhou Bay to the south there are 50 or more excellent boats for hire.

Most deep-sea fishing is done by trolling in water of 1000 fathoms (1800m; 6000ft) or less, although

along the drop-offs on the Kona coast, boats troll for marlin and tuna in waters up to 2000 fathoms (3600m; 12,000ft). Kona holds blue marlin records in a number of line classes, including 624.14kg (1376 lb) in the 60kg (130 lb) class and two marlin over 500kg (1103 lb) in lighter classes, taken off Kailua-Kona.

Big-game fishing in Hawaii is not limited to the Kona coast however. Off Oahu, the most populated island, charterboats fish close inshore as well as offshore for marlin, yellowfin tuna (known locally as *ahi*), wahoo (*ono*), and dolphinfish (*mahi mahi*).

On Oahu, boats are available from Honolulu, as well as Waianae, Kewalo Basin, Haleiwa and Heeia Kea harbours. Charterboats can also be found at Maalaea and Lahaina harbours on Maui, Kaunakakai on Molokai and Manele Bay on Lanai.

Due to the popularity of Hawaii as a big-game fishing destination, a number of international billfish tournaments are held throughout the year and noncompeting anglers intending to visit the 50th state should enquire well in advance about the availability of charterboats and accommodation.

Above and left *The islands of Hawaii offer some of the best big-game fishing in the world, especially off the Kona coast of the 'Big Island'.*

NORTH AND SOUTH CAROLINA

The Gulf Stream runs along the coast of the Carolinas and there is some good marlin fishing off Cape Hatteras, North Carolina.

Charterboats are available at many towns and much of the coast offers sheltered inlets and bays. Anglers can fish for yellowfin and blackfin tuna, blue marlin (some record specimens have been taken off Cape Hatteras and Oregan Inlet), sailfish and oceanic bonito, all of which have also been caught south of Wrightsville beach.

A number of angling tournaments are held in both states, mainly in the summer months. In the mid-1990s, a new giant bluefin tuna fishery was discovered off Hatteras. The 68–227kg (150–500 lb) tuna are caught mostly from December to February.

THE NORTHEASTERN SEABOARD

Taking in Virginia, Maryland, Delaware, New Jersey, New York and the New England states, this area of the western Atlantic is not known to produce monster fish, but white marlin, swordfish, tuna, black drum and mako shark can be found here.

Throughout the region, saltwater fly and light tackle fishing are popular in the calmer inshore areas and species taken by these methods include striped bass, bluefish and bonito.

The coastline of New Jersey has numerous river mouths and creeks while offshore, the continental shelf is strewn with wrecks and reefs, just the place for foodfish and the big predators that feed on them.

New York harbour is an unlikely spot to catch large tuna, but in late summer there is a run of these fish, which are caught using live bluefish as bait.

A reasonable drive from the 'Big Apple' takes one to Long Island, where charterboats are available from Montauk Harbour to take anglers offshore to seek bluefin and big-eye tuna, and billfish, in the Atlantic, where a number of record specimens have been captured. Bluefin tuna are also trolled off Cape Cod in Massachusetts, and from the nearby resorts of Martha's Vineyard and Nantucket, where record white marlin have been taken. Shark fishing is popular with many anglers off the northeast US coast.

Rhode Island, the smallest state, hosts the annual United States Atlantic Tuna Tournament, fished out of Point Judith Pond. One notable event saw the capture of 34 bluefin tuna with their combined weight reaching 8098.4kg (17,854 lb), 20 of them having individual weights over 226.7kg (500 lb), and the biggest one tipping the scales at 343.8kg (758 lb).

The biggest tuna arrive in midsummer (July to August) and are gone by November. The area also offers white and blue marlin and swordfish.

Charterboats are readily available throughout the eastern seaboard states, with most operations offering a choice of deep-sea or inshore fishing.

ALASKA

Salmon is the mainstay of Alaska's fishing industry, with all five species of Pacific salmon occuring here. Bottomfish, including halibut and flounder, are also abundant, but many of the prime areas are relatively inaccessible to recreational anglers. A number of record Pacific halibut have been taken off the

Alaskan coast, with the top weight recorded being 208.2kg (459 lb) from Dutch Harbor on the Alaskan Peninsula. The many islands and inlets of southern Alaska and the Alaskan Peninsula hold most of the class records for this species.

CANADA

While Canada's salmon fishing rivers are superlative, and deep-sea fishing for salmon and halibut takes place in the Pacific off British Columbia, true saltwater game fishing is pursued only by those who live on or near the coasts, for distances are huge.

Bluefin tuna and swordfish can be found in the cold Atlantic waters off the eastern provinces of Nova Scotia and Newfoundland. A record bluefin tuna of 679kg (1496 lb) was caught off Aulds Cove, Nova Scotia, in 1979, but in recent years these fish appear to have moved away, no doubt as a result of commercial overfishing. Large bluefin tuna have been taken around Prince Edward Island in the Gulf of St Lawrence off Newfoundland, including a woman's record of 530.7kg (1170 lb).

There are angling centres at a number of towns, including Cape St Mary, Junt's Point and Queen's County in Nova Scotia, but anglers may have difficulty finding deep-sea boats, as much of Canada's charter industry is concentrated on salmon.

MEXICO

Mexico's sport-fishing industry has grown enormously in recent years and the country is poised to exploit to the full its new-found popularity as a game fishing destination. Anglers have a choice of locations, from the vibrant resort towns on the Yucatán Peninsula in the Gulf of Mexico to the comparative isolation of Baja California on the Pacific coast. Cabo San Lucas, at the southernmost tip of Baja California, is a world class fishing centre. (Baja, in northwest Mexico, is often mistakenly assumed to be part of the United States.) It is a hot, arid region with beautiful mountains and a picturesque seashore.

Above *Baja California in Mexico offers excellent big-game fishing.*
Left *Fishing for bluefin tuna off the eastern seaboard of the USA.*

Mexico's more than 9000km (5600 miles) of coastline is rich in big-game species such as blue marlin, yellowfin tuna, wahoo, roosterfish and yellowtail, with each coast offering its own distinct species. A number of record yellowfin tuna have been taken off the islands in the Gulf of California, with the top weight of 176.3kg (388 lb) taken off Isla San Benedicto. Commercial fishing is beginning to take off, with the main catches being tuna, anchovies, sardines and mackerel.

For big-game fishermen, the key angling centres are on the Pacific coast and include La Paz, the capital of Baja California, and Cabo San Lucas. The smaller towns of Mulegé and Loreto, both former mission stations, boast a number of fishing lodges and are an ideal starting point for visiting the many islands in the Gulf of California (also called the Mar de Cortés, or Sea of Cortez).

The sea off Cabo San Lucas teems with fish and the town, supported by a good charter industry, has become internationally renowned as a year-round game fishing destination. Whale-watching is another popular tourist attraction here, as each year, California grey whales gather on Baja's Pacific coast to mate and calve in the sheltered bays, lagoons and coves near the towns of Guerrero Negro, Laguna San Ignacio and Isla Magdalena.

Mazatlán is a busy commercial and fishing port on the Pacific and a popular beach resort. From here, as well as from Acapulco, anglers can go out for sailfish, swordfish, shark and tarpon. Further south, the tourist resorts of Ixtapa and Zihuatanejo offer a range of watersports, including deep-sea fishing.

On the opposite side of the country, the Yucatán Peninsula is bounded by the Caribbean and the Gulf of Mexico. The key destination for anglers is the resort city of Cancún on the eastern coast. With its pleasant year-round climate, turquoise waters and white sands, Cancún is a popular tourist centre for travellers from Europe and the USA and angling visitors will find that they are well catered for. There are a number of reefs off Cancún and the nearby Cozumel and Mujeres islands are a haven for snorkellers and scuba divers.

An indication of the growing importance of Mexico as an international angling destination was the decision by the European Federation of Sea Anglers (EFSA) to hold their 1997 Game Fishing Championships at Puerto Vallarta, situated in the Bahía de Banderas on the Pacific coast.

During the championships 23 dorado, 17 wahoo, 104 bonito, 109 skipjack, 38 sailfish, eight sharks, five roosterfish and a barracuda were caught. Two prize catches were a 104kg (229 lb) yellowfin tuna, and a wahoo of 13.75kg (29 lb).

The Marina Vallarta is a development with luxury accommodation and slips for some 300 boats. Here fishermen go to sea daily to gather the fish that are part of the staple diet of the local inhabitants.

THE CARIBBEAN AND CENTRAL AMERICA

The islands of the Caribbean and western Atlantic include Bermuda, the Bahamas, Jamaica, Haiti, Puerto Rico, Cuba, the Caymans, the British and US Virgin Islands, Turks and Caicos and the Dominican Republic. While information on Bermuda, the Bahamas, Jamaica, Puerto Rico and other islands is

readily available, anglers wishing to fish in Haiti, Cuba and the Dominican Republic should first contact the various tourist agencies and embassies.

The Central American countries Costa Rica, Panama, Belize, Guatemala, Honduras, El Salvador and Nicaragua are located on the isthmus which joins the continents of North and South America.

BERMUDA

Situated in the Atlantic 1610km (1000 miles) north of the Caribbean and brushed by the warm waters of the Gulf Stream, Bermuda offers excellent big-game fishing all year round, with the best times between May and November. The islands also boast the world's most northerly coral reefs.

Blue and white marlin, four tunas (blackfin, yellowfin, bluefin and skipjack), dolphinfish, barracuda, greater amberjack, wahoo and Atlantic sailfish are all found off Bermuda. Local angler and charter captain Alan Card has caught three blue marlin weighing over 1000 lb (453.5kg).

A number of record blackfin tuna (also known as Bermuda tuna or blackfinned albacore) have been taken, although this small species rarely reaches the weights of its heavier relatives. It is an ideal fish for light tackle casting with small baits, lures or feathers and can also be taken by live-bait fishing in deep waters a few kilometres offshore. This lively fish makes good eating, but the Bermudan authorities' request that most big-game fish be returned alive to the water is to be commended, as it ensures the on-going future of the sport.

Two saltwater fly fishing records for yellowfin tuna have also been recorded off Bermuda.

A game fishing tournament is held by the Bermuda Department of Tourism each year between April and November. Anglers wishing to participate should enquire well in advance, particularly if they wish to charter.

Charterboats can be hired for full or half-days and rates are dependent on the number of anglers. All fishing tackle is included in the cost.

Above *The natural harbour at Charlotte Amalie, St Thomas, US Virgin Islands.*
Left *The essence of the Caribbean is captured in the blue skies and turquoise seas of the Virgin Islands.*

Above *The fishing is good on both the windward and leeward coasts off Bimini in the Bahamas.*
Right *A variety of big-game fish can be found off Montego Bay, Jamaica.*

BAHAMAS

This archipelago of some 700 islands lies in the shallow waters of Great Bahama Bank and other smaller banks which spread out around them.

The tourism industry is thriving, and with good reason, for the climate is just what the angler or holidaymaker wants, and Miami is only 80km (50 miles) away. Summers are warm to hot with temperatures in the 27–32°C (80–90°F) range and winters average 21°C (70°F), although they can drop to a slightly chilly 9°C (49°F).

The big-game angler visiting this archipelago is spoilt for choice. Twenty-one of the more than 50 IGFA-acknowledged big-game species occur here, so those who specialize in any one group or even a single species can have the trip of a lifetime.

There is no clash, either, between commercial boats, which take shellfish, lobsters, turtles and the smaller fish, and sportfishermen who are after the much larger fish such as marlin, tuna, tarpon, sail-

fish, wahoo, amberjack, dolphinfish and barracuda. Bimini holds a number of records for white marlin and in the mid-1990s a 454.5kg (1000 lb) blue marlin was taken at Treasure Cay, in the northeast Bahamas.

One of the prime places for barracuda is Walker's Cay, where these fang-toothed torpedoes are found both on the surface and at the bottom.

Of all the angling centres in the Bahamas, Bimini is the prime venue, with a dozen billfish tournaments organized every year off the Great Bahama Bank. A number of marinas, including Brown's, Weech's Bimini Dock, Bahamas Big Game Fishing Club and Blue Water, offer charterboats for hire, with costs depending on the size of craft. At least three hotels on Andros have their own charterboats.

Ernest Hemingway, who caught a large bluefin tuna off Bimini, called it his favourite angling centre. His last novel *Islands in the Stream,* which is set here, includes an epic story of a young boy's fight with a thousand-pound broadbill.

JAMAICA

In the Caribbean, 145km (90 miles) south of Cuba, lies the island of Jamaica, the waters of which are home to blue marlin, dolphinfish, wahoo and bonito, to name a few. In Jamaica, it is not the size but the abundance of fish that attracts big-game anglers, although a local fisherman in a canoe is said to have caught a blue marlin weighing 272kg (600 lb).

Jamaica has been described as a 'pelagic playpen' for dolphinfish, tuna and wahoo. This is due to the varied seabed and the currents sweeping around undersea 'mountains' that reach almost to the water's surface and provide a home for feeding fish.

Some excellent fishing areas can be reached easily from the capital, Kingston. However, on the northern side of the island, Montego Bay faces the deep waters of the off-shore Cayman Trench, which lies between Jamaica and Cuba. This area has been called 'Marlin Alley', due to the prevalence of blue marlin fish in these waters.

There are seven blue marlin tournaments held in Jamaica every year, the biggest and best of which is the Port Antonio International, which takes place in October. The delightfully named Blue Water Angling Club, near Whitehouse, also holds an annual international game fishing tournament.

Anglers not wanting to go too far out can fish for tarpon at Falmouth, on the north coast.

CAYMAN ISLANDS

Head south about 240km (150 miles) from Cuba and the little dots on the map reveal themselves to be the Cayman Islands, divided into the Grand and the Little Caymans.

These popular tourist islands, part of the Greater Antilles, are protected by surrounding reefs, just outside of which are plenty of blue marlin, the prime big-game fishing attraction, and many other species, including wahoo and tuna. Tarpon can also be found in the brackish water of the inshore flats.

PUERTO RICO

The easternmost of the Greater Antilles, Puerto Rico has the Atlantic to its north and the Caribbean to its south. More than 60 big-game species occur here, including marlin and yellowfin tuna, which are taken by trolling with both natural baits and lures.

Blue and white marlin are permanent inhabitants off the Atlantic coast. The women's blue marlin record in the 10kg (20 lb) class, at 181.89kg (410 lb), was taken off San Juan, and for a time the island also held the men's record for blue marlin, although this has now been superseded. Club Nautico de San Juan is a centre for big-game fishing and sponsors a world-class blue marlin tournament each summer. Off the east coast lie the Grappers Banks, which have been described as a 'wahoo paradise'.

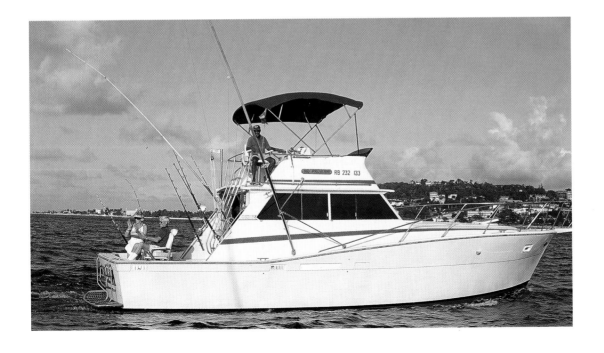

Coral Bay in the US Virgin Islands is an attractive game fishing destination for blue marlin, tuna and wahoo.

VIRGIN ISLANDS

These popular tourist islands, part of the Lesser Antilles and lying south of Puerto Rico, belong to both the US and the UK. The game-fishing industry is centred on St Thomas in the US Virgin Islands.

The sport-fishing season starts in May with summer fishing for sailfish, black- and yellowfin tuna, blue marlin and wahoo. Some 20 world records, many for blue marlin, have been taken off St Thomas, including a notable woman's record for blue marlin of 486.7kg (1073 lb).

There is a thriving charterboat industry out of the US islands of St Thomas and St Croix, while many visitors to the British Virgin Islands stay on their own boats. As expected of a top tourist destination, facilities are often luxurious and anglers wishing to visit should enquire about prices in advance to avoid a nasty shock at the end of the trip.

BELIZE

Belize (formerly British Honduras) lies just south of the Yucatán Peninsula in Mexico. Facing the Caribbean Sea, big-game species are as abundant off this coast as they are elsewhere in the region.

Much of the game fishing activity focuses on the offshore Turneffe Island and Ambergris Cay. There is an active charter industry, offering facilities for serious fishing for blue marlin, king mackerel, sailfish and barracuda, all of which are found in this area as their food-fish are plentiful.

PANAMA

New Zealand angler Zane Grey was one of the first to explore the seas here in search of big fish. Today, Panama offers anglers a choice of the Caribbean or Pacific coast, and most of the big-game fish occur here including black marlin, amberjack and wahoo.

The Club de Pesca in Pinas Bay records an average of 15 marlin contacts a day. Pacific sailfish can be taken on whole bonito (which suggests the size you can expect). The Tropic Star Lodge at Pinas Bay is one of several fishing centres in Panama.

COSTA RICA

Costa Rica, which claims to be the sailfish capital of the world, is situated on the narrow isthmus that joins North and South America, and like Panama, offers both Pacific and Caribbean coastlines.

THE INTERNATIONAL GAME FISH ASSOCIATION (IGFA)

The world's most important game fish authority, with affiliated clubs, associations and federations on every continent, the IGFA was founded in 1939 at the American Museum of History in New York to monitor and keep world game fish records and administer the rules of the sport. IGFA's many roles include maintaining a research database, a museum of fishing and a library of 8000 books on fishing topics.

Annual membership of the IGFA costs US$25 (USA members); US$30 (foreign members); US$35 (USA family); US$40 (foreign family). Life membership can be obtained for US$1000*.

Members receive a membership card, plus the very informative annual book of World Record Game Fishes, a bimonthly newsletter about international angling worldwide and an embroidered IGFA official badge. Established angling clubs around the world are able to apply for club membership, at a fee of US$40 (for both USA national clubs and foreign clubs). Individual and affiliated member clubs are widespread and provide a useful source of contacts for anglers travelling abroad.
*All costs quoted at 1999 rates.

CLAIMING A WORLD RECORD

Any claim for the capture of a world record rod-caught fish undergoes stringent checking. The fish must have been caught according to IGFA rules, must be a species commonly fished for with rod and line, and must be clearly identifiable based on photographs and supporting data.

In order to reflect the value of a large fish taken on comparatively light line tackle, the IGFA instituted a range of line classes. All applications must be accompanied by a US$10 (membership) or US$25 (nonmembership) fee.

The regulations for record claims are complex, and any angler with records in mind should obtain all the relevant information from IGFA.

Under the IGFA aegis, tag and release programmes are under way in many countries throughout the world.

International Game Fish Association
300 Gulf Stream Way, Dania
Florida 33004 USA
Tel + 954 927-2628
Website: http://www.igfa.org
e-mail: IGFAHQ@aol.com

The fighting ability and spectacular aerial acrobatics of the sailfish as it performs barrel rolls and graceful leaps out of the water offers an unforgettable experience for the angler who hooks one. Although the record books list two types of sailfish, Atlantic and Pacific, there is some debate as to whether they are different species. In addition to sailfish records, Costa Rica holds an IGFA record for dolphinfish, with a 39.4kg (87 lb) specimen from Papagallo Gulf on the Pacific coast.

Charterboats are available from Flamingo Bay, El Ocatal and Golfito.

Above and right *Recognizing the importance of adventure tourism, Brazilian authorities are actively promoting their country as a major big-game fishing destination.*

SOUTH AMERICA

Distances on this huge continent are vast, but the big-game angler can test his skills on either the Atlantic and Pacific oceans, as the seas on both coasts of South America offer tremendous big-game angling. Game fishing is not all that well organized in many South American countries, and anglers wishing to try these waters should obtain as much advance information as possible.

VENEZUELA

The sportfishing scene in this Caribbean-facing country seems to be reasonably well organized and there are plenty of game fish species, including blue and white marlin, sailfish, swordfish, bluefin tuna, dolphinfish and bonito. There are opportunities for deep-sea fishing using heavy tackle, as well as light tackle and saltwater fly fishing. Many of the best skippers work commercially and anglers intending to visit Venezuela should enquire beforehand about the availability of charterboats.

BRAZIL

There are plenty of opportunities for big-game fishing along Brazil's extensive Atlantic coast and the government seems to want to promote the sport.

White and blue marlin abound, and Vitoria, which lies north of Rio de Janeiro, holds a number of white marlin records in various classes, including an 82.5kg (182 lb) specimen. A new marlin fishery has been developed in the northeast of the country. At Cabo Frio, a little way north of Rio de Janeiro, sailfish have been taken. Brazil also has fishing for tarpon and bluefish.

ARGENTINA

The world's eighth largest country is a trout fisherman's heaven, and all the guidebooks concentrate on this branch of fishing. What the Atlantic offers in big-game fishing off Argentina is less certain, although a record dorado of 23.3kg (51 lb 5oz) was caught off Toledo.

The warm Brazil Current sweeps southwards, meeting the cold Falklands Current on its way up from the Antarctic. Although there are some big-game species to be found off the Falklands Islands, as well as an established commercial pelagic fishery, conditions in these southerly waters can be harsh for much of the year.

CHILE

This long, mountainous country has a 4584km (2600-mile) stretch of Pacific coastline, from the Tropic of Capricorn in the north, to Patagonia and Tierra del Fuego in the south, where subzero temperatures on sea and land are the norm.

A great deal of the Chilean economy is based on the sea and the country's thriving pelagic fish industry is a major source of income and employment. Most of the larger coastal towns have fishing interests, and yellowfin tuna are harvested commercially.

Iquique, in the north, is the main port for recreational angling. A swordfish of 536.15kg (1182 lb) was caught here, although commercial fishermen from Antofagasta and Tocopilla are known to have landed bigger specimens.

Chile's impressive list of big-game fish, which includes sailfish in the north, as well as the elusive broadbill swordfish, known locally as *albacora* or *pez espada*, owes its existence to the presence of the cold Humboldt (also called the Peru) Current, which flows westwards around Cape Horn and then northwards, carrying with it the squid, sardines and anchovies that attract game fish.

Other large big-game fish species occurring off Chile include black marlin, which tend to keep to the warmer currents. Striped marlin, which have been reported up to 136kg (300 lb), yellowfin, skipjacks and other tuna (the big-eye tops the weights) are taken. There are also sharks, notably the blue shark.

CHAPTER SEVEN

EUROPE

S ea temperatures in Europe vary greatly, from the predominantly chilly English Channel and North Sea to the more southerly and therefore warmer seas round the Iberian Peninsula and in the near tideless Mediterranean. These temperature differences naturally have an effect on the big-game fish species the angler can expect to find. Although most big-game fish live in subtropical and tropical waters, when sea temperatures rise in waters that are normally cool, such as during a long hot spell, there can be incursions of 'exotic' species.

The Gulf Stream that originates in the Caribbean sweeps through the eastern Atlantic, bringing warmer water to the islands of the Azores, Madeira and the Canaries, and it is here that some of the continent's best big-game fishing is found.

With global warming, the northerly seas around Europe may well see more warm-water species coming into areas where they are currently unknown.

THE AZORES

The Azores, an archipelago of nine volcanic islands belonging to Portugal, are situated in the mid-Atlantic, on the 39th parallel. Some 20 years ago, sea temperatures in this area rose, resulting in an increase in warm-water-loving game fish.

The big-game fleet operates out of Horta on Faial Island and fishes the famed Condor Bank for blue marlin that can top 453.5kg (1000 lb). A world record of 520kg (1146 lb) was taken here in 1988.

However, since US fishermen 'discovered' the Azores, increased demand has pushed the price of big-game charterboats to over US$1000 a day.

The deep waters around these steep volcanic islands also attract sharks, including mako, blue,

Some of the best big-game fishing in Europe takes place out of Horta, on Faial Island in the Azores.

hammerhead and whitetip sharks of awesome proportions. The giant six-gilled shark can be taken inshore by deep fishing with bait. Bluefin tuna weighing up to 318kg (700 lb) are also caught, plus an increasing number of white marlin, which can be found in the vicinity of Santa Maria, one of the other islands in the archipelago.

CANARY ISLANDS

This group of Spanish holiday islands in the sub-tropical Atlantic, off the west coast of Africa, is where European big-game fishing first took off. There is a very well-established fleet of boats at Las Palmas on Gran Canaria but, like the other European deep-water Atlantic islands, it is important

THE EUROPEAN FEDERATION OF SEA ANGLERS (EFSA)

Formed in 1961, EFSA has 20 member countries worldwide. It serves as the governing body for the sport of sea angling with rod and line in European waters and as keeper of the European record fish list of marine species.

EFSA's annual European Sea Angling Championships have taken place in different countries (Gibraltar, Scotland, Iceland, France, Norway, Wales, England, Sweden, Holland and Denmark) each year since 1962.

Recent EFSA championships include the European Tope Festival, held in Tenby, Wales, the European Cod Festival, also held in Wales and the Game Fishing Championships, held out of Hout Bay, Cape Town, South Africa

Previous Game Fishing Championships have taken place in Kenya, Florida and Mexico.

Individual EFSA members are entitled to become associate members of the International Game Fish Association (IGFA).

Mr H.R. Holmes, Secretary, EFSA
Inglewood, Braal Road, Halkirk
Caithness KW12 6EX, Scotland
Tel + 44 1847 83-1524
Fax + 44 1955 60-2481
www.cornwall-online.co.uk/efsa

Above *Sharks are frequently caught off the Algarve coast in southern Portugal.*

to time your visit to coincide with when the fish are running close to the shore on their annual migrations. Unlike the Caribbean islands, there are no banks or areas of shallow water around the Canary Islands to hold the game fish in the area for long.

World record big-eye tuna of more than 136kg (300 lb) have been taken during the summer months, notably between June and August, just 9km (6 miles) out on the first drop-off, while big wahoo are caught by inshore trolling with jet lures.

July and August are when the first run of giant blue marlin passes through these waters. If you are lucky enough to hook one, it is likely to be big. A woman's 24kg (50 lb) line class world record of 364kg (802 lb) was taken back in 1986, but since then much larger fish of around 454.5kg (1000 lb) have been caught on lures.

During the last couple of years, a number of charterboats have been fishing the sea between the islands of Tenerife and Gomera. Catches have included blue marlin to 408kg (900 lb), as well as wahoo, big-eye tuna, dorado and skipjack.

MADEIRA

The picturesque island of Madeira, which lies southwest of Portugal, is another popular European game fishing destination.

Blue marlin of more than 454.5kg (1000 lb) have been taken, on a tag and release basis, just a few kilometres offshore in the deep waters that result from the sudden drop-off surrounding these volcanic islands. The European rod-caught marlin record of 550.2kg (1212 lb) comes from these waters.

Like the Azores, the crucial time to hit these migratory fish is July to October. The blue marlin can reach weights as high as 272kg (600 lb) and are taken by fast trolling with lures.

Madeira is renowned for its run of big-eye tuna from March until May. These average between 23kg (50 lb) and 90kg (200 lb) and are the subject of a large commercial fishing operation.

Large wahoo and dolphinfish also run close inshore in summer and yellowfin tuna, albacore, swordfish, barracuda, hammerhead and mako sharks can be found here.

PORTUGAL

The southern Algarve coastline is truly the new frontier of European big-game fishing, with the deep waters of the Atlantic in easy reach of Sagres, Faro, Lagos and other ports.

The area is famed for its sharks, including large blue shark of more than 90kg (200 lb), hammerheads of 136kg (300 lb) and makos. Bluefin tuna and swordfish up to 227kg (500 lb) are taken on rod and line from long-range commercial fishing boats operating out of Sagres and Sesimbra.

In the mid-1990s, pioneering boats discovered the presence of blue marlin within comfortable reach of the shore. So far, three blue marlin of more than 454.5kg (1000 lb) have been taken, as well as a number reaching the 181kg (400 lb) mark.

In 1997 large shoals of white marlin were discovered a few miles offshore from Tavira, near the Spanish border. A tournament in September 1998 resulted in the capture of 40 white marlin weighing up to 54kg (119 lb), taken on trolled lures, with some boats enjoying up to 30 strikes a day.

The Algarve coast enjoys some sensational shark fishing, thanks to the vast shoals of sprat, pilchard and other baitfish found in the shallow inshore waters which serve as a shark nursery. Most fish taken will be small pups, which should be returned alive, but anglers can expect the big females as well. Fly fishing from a drifting boat for blue shark and small makos is becoming popular.

As the eastern Atlantic appears to be warming up, expect to find more game species such as skipjack, dolphinfish and big-eye tuna. Bluefish are also found along the rocky coastline, along with the legendary giant sea bass.

GIBRALTAR

Seven different ocean currents meet in the Strait of Gibraltar, making it one of the most dramatic and dangerous places in Europe for deep-sea fishing.

In the last five years, there have been serious attempts to open 'the Rock' up for big-game fishing, particularly since the political climate between Spain and the UK has improved over its disputed waters.

BRITISH RECORD FISH COMMITTEE (BRFC)

The BRFC was founded 40 years ago when an angling newspaper started publishing 'biggest fish' stories and a 'league table' of the top rod-caught weights of fresh- and saltwater fish species.

It keeps strict lists of the best recorded and authenticated weights throughout the British Isles and the Channel Islands.

51a Queen Street, Newton Abbot
Devon TQ12 2QJ, England
Tel + 44 01626 33-1330.

Above *This 324kg (714 lb) blue marlin was taken off the Azores in 1986.*
Left *The seas beneath the dramatic cliffs of Gibraltar's famous rock are dangerous, but offer good fishing.*

Since the Spanish fleets stopped commercial netting for the bluefin tuna which run past Gibraltar on their way into the Mediterranean, the fishing for them has improved tenfold. Fast trolling with lures in March and April results in bluefin averaging 14–23kg (30–50 lb), but later in the year fish weighing more than 136kg (300 lb) are taken on the other side of the Strait, off the Spanish African coast at Cueta. Bonito arrive in September and stay until April.

White marlin are also now being caught, while swordfish have been baited on the surface out in the Strait during the day. Deep fishing with wire line can produce scabbard fish, grouper and six-gilled shark.

The Gibraltans regularly hold international sea-fishing competitions and the author has enjoyed many a day out in boats from the old quay while taking part in the annual Gibraltar Shark Angling Festival, when fair-sized shark have been brought in. This is organized by EFSA's Gibraltar section.

SPAIN

Despite having both Atlantic and Mediterranean coastlines, the author is not aware of any seriously organized deep-sea fishing here, although for some years Spain has concentrated on developing a considerable amount of freshwater fishing.

Tagging records show however that bluefin, big-eye and skipjack tuna and albacore have been captured by scientists and commerical fishermen in the Bay of Biscay on the Atlantic coast.

At Castellón de la Plana, on the Mediterranean coast north of Valencia, Club Nautico hosts the annual Spanish International Tuna Championships.

The port of Marbella, on the Costa del Sol, has at least one charter operation which goes out for bluefin tuna, shark or large bottomfish such as grouper. Some of the coastal areas, such as the Costa Brava (rocky coast) near the French border, attract many local and tourist rock anglers.

IRELAND

The Gulf Stream sweeps up along the continental shelf to the south and west of Ireland, bringing rich warm water that supports large stocks of food-fish. Their presence makes for grand angling in the Irish Republic, where geology, weather and water combine to make any angling trip an enjoyable event.

Such is the interest in sea fishing in the Emerald Isle that many coastal towns, including Dungarvan and Kinsale in the south and Portrush in Northern Ireland, have fishing centres. Belmullet, on the west coast, has good boats for hire and charter.

At Kinsale in County Cork, blue shark hover above the wreck of the *Lusitania*, torpedoed off the Old Head during World War I. The nearby towns of Cobh, Courtmacsherry and Cork Harbour also offer some worthwhile fishing.

Westport, in County Mayo, holds an international sea-angling event each year. Blue shark to over 90kg (200 lb), porbeagle to over 163kg (360 lb) and six-gilled shark up to 70kg (154 lb) are all taken here. Commercial boats take bluefin tuna off the west coast, but they are too far out for most charterboats.

The Irish Tourist Board can offer advice on fishing, boats, bait, tackle and accommodation. The Irish Specimen Fish Committee, based in Dublin, is a useful source of information on fishing in Eire.

Ireland is famous for its hospitality, but if you start a conversation about fishing in a local bar, your chances of getting out early diminish by the glass and you could find yourself in deeper water than the fish you hope to catch!

ENGLAND AND WALES

The seeker of big-game fish in England will, of necessity, confine his fishing to the southwest corner of the country, where the warm waters of the Gulf Stream have the most effect (the author has experienced the oddity of dipping his hands into the frigid English Channel to warm them, the water being warmer than the ambient temperature of the air!).

Plymouth, in Devon, is the major deep-sea angling centre in the south of England. From here, boats take anglers to the Eddystone Light and Hands Deep, as well as on two- or three-day trips out to well-known wrecks in the area.

Opposite *Anglers seeking bluefin tuna in the Mediterranean put to sea from harbours such as this one in southern France.*
Below *A blue shark is gaffed prior to being brought to the boat in the English Channel off the Cornwall coast.*

The village of Looe, in Cornwall, is home to the Shark Angling Club of Great Britain. Other fishing centres can be found at Mevagissey and Falmouth in Cornwall, around the Bristol Channel and off the west coast of Wales.

A number of large sharks have been taken off Cornwall, including a blue of 99kg (218 lb), mako of 227kg (500 lb) and porbeagle of 211kg (465 lb). A sunfish of 49kg (108 lb) has also been caught. An unusual catch some years ago was a small 4kg (9 lb) six-gilled shark, well out of its area. The record for this species, 485kg (1069 lb) was taken off the Azores. In southern England, just into the English Channel proper, a thresher shark of 146kg (323 lb) was taken off Portsmouth.

Before World War II, in 1930, L Mitchell Henry and Col. R F Stapleton-Cotton set out on a few game fishing trips into the North Sea from Scarborough in Yorkshire. To their surprise they encountered some very heavy fish which they were not expecting and consequently lost. Intrigued, they returned the following year armed with heavier tackle and proceeded to catch a 227kg (500 lb) bluefin tuna. For the next nine years a steady catch of bluefin was made, culminating in a British record weight of 386kg (851 lb).

The stocks have since been decimated by commercial fishing and bluefin tuna were last taken here in 1954. In recent years, North Sea trawlers have netted giant porbeagle sharks and swordfish, proving their existence in cooler waters.

SCOTLAND

The scenic mountainous coast of western Scotland, the Inner and Outer Hebrides, the Orkneys and associated islands are all touched by the Gulf Stream, although it is rather cool by the time it has flowed this far north. Nevertheless, Scottish records do show some considerable specimens, notably a common skate of 103kg (227 lb).

Halibut are found around the Orkney and Shetland Islands off the northern tip of Scotland. Among the largest bony fish in the sea, they reach weights of 317kg (700 lb) here. The Scottish (and UK) rod-caught record halibut of 106kg (234 lb) was taken off northeast Scotland, where the coastlines of Caithness and the Orkney Islands also provide some great porbeagle shark fishing.

THE CHANNEL ISLES

The islands of Guernsey, Jersey, Alderney and Sark are autonomous British territories and easily reached by ferry from either England or France. Their location close to the French coast, in warmer southerly waters, gives anglers here an edge on those fishing the cooler northern side of the English Channel.

There is good boat-fishing to be had around the rocky coastlines of these islands. A blue shark of 54kg (120 lb) and a porbeagle shark of 99kg (220 lb) were taken off Guernsey, while Jersey held the British porbeagle record of 195kg (430 lb), before it was beaten by one taken off Padstowe in Cornwall that weighed 211kg (465 lb).

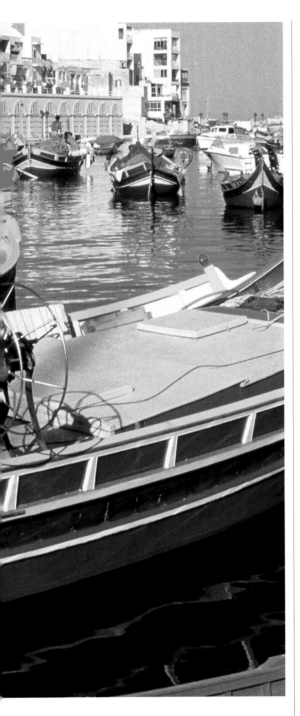

The Atlantic offers a fairly unusual species, the meagre, which reaches 65kg (143 lb), and occurs in the southern area of the Bay of Biscay on the west coast. Various tunas, including the albacore and skipjack, are also taken in these waters.

Close to the Spanish border, local deep-sea anglers go out from Port de Boue where they range about 15km (9 miles) out to sea to seek bluefin tuna, which reach weights from 90 kg (200 lb) up to 136kg (300 lb). Small bluefin tuna are also found eastwards along the coast, in the Golfe de Genes.

The Monaco Game Fishing Club organizes an annual International Tuna Championship, which takes place off Monte Carlo. An annual shark festival in the 10kg (20 lb) line class is organized by the French section of the EFSA.

The French island of Corsica has a large commercial fishing fleet, but there is not much information on recreational game fishing here.

MALTA

A former British colony, the four islands of Malta are situated in one of the most favourable areas of the Mediterranean for big-game fishing, which is now beginning to play an important part in the country's many attractions.

Tuna, dolphinfish and amberjack, which are trolled for, are known in the seas surrounding these historic islands, which also has sharks, including the great white, and a variety of inshore species.

There are reports of broadbill swordfish being taken by the many commercial fishermen that operate from Malta, but recreational anglers have not yet begun to take this species on rod and reel.

SCANDINAVIA AND ICELAND

The fishing in these colder northern countries tends to focus on salmon, although some large deep-sea species are found in the rocky fjords of Norway and off the coast of Sweden.

A bluefin tuna weighing 371kg (818 lb) is listed in Danish fishing records. A Greenland shark of 361kg (796 lb) was caught in Norway's Beistadfjord in Norway, as were ling up to 30kg (66 lb). Although not considered big-game fish, ling are not to be sneered at if taken on light tackle. Iceland's waters are normally too cold for traditional big-game fishing, but some large halibut have been caught there.

FRANCE

With a coastline that takes in the English Channel, the Atlantic Ocean and the Mediterranean, French fishermen have a wide choice of ports and harbours from which to go deep-sea fishing, although the best big-game fishing opportunities are to be found in the warmer waters of the Mediterranean.

Opposite *Traditional fishing boats in the harbour at St Julian's, north of Valetta, the capital of Malta.*

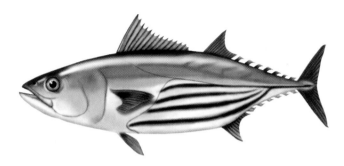

CHAPTER EIGHT

AFRICA AND AUSTRALASIA

AFRICA

This huge continent, bounded by the Atlantic and Indian oceans and the Mediterranean and Red seas, cannot be treated as a whole. Geographically and culturally diverse, the continent's vast coastline offers several big-game fishing alternatives.

Two countries – South Africa and Kenya – dominate the scene at present, but changing political circumstances are opening up exciting opportunities for deep-sea anglers looking for a challenge and a variety of new experiences.

Those with a sense of adventure are heading for Mozambique and Madagascar, while anglers looking for tropical sunshine and warm seas turn to the Seychelles and the other Indian Ocean islands.

SOUTH AFRICA

The coastline of South Africa extends nearly 2000km (1200 miles) from the Orange River in the west to Mozambique on the east coast, rounding Cape Agulhas, the southernmost tip of Africa, on the way. Situated as it is between the Atlantic and Indian oceans, South Africa is uniquely placed for both cold and warm water angling.

Two separate currents and their prevailing ecosystems influence the variety and availability of the large number of big-game and other fish species found in South African waters.

The west coast is dominated by the north-flowing cold Benguela Current that originates in Antarctic waters and feeds in through submarine canyons, with its starting point at Cape Point, one of Cape Town's famous landmarks (the other being Table Mountain). This current provides the nutrient-rich water that is the primary source of huge plankton

The dramatic headland of Cape Point marks the divide between the warm Agulhas and cold Benguela currents.

blooms which, in turn, support great concentrations of pelagic fish such as anchovy, pilchard and hake. However, due to the relatively cool water, only a few different species occur in this area and big-game fish are not normally encountered.

By contrast, South Africa's east coast offers a sub-tropical ecosystem, nurtured by the warm Agulhas Current which originates in the equatorial waters of the Indian Ocean. This powerful current flows close to the coast in a southwesterly direction, turning off-shore at Cape Agulhas. A variety of fish species, often brilliantly coloured, are found along this coast-line. Big-game fish, including billfish and tunas, occur in the warm east coast waters.

The coast between Cape Agulhas and Cape Point is a transition area, with the cold Benguela Current dominating in the winter months (May to September) and the warmer Agulhas waters in spring and summer. Game fish such as tuna undertake seasonal migrations to this part of the coast to feed on the abundant bait-fish trailing the edges of the plankton-rich water. The mystical broadbill swordfish is known to congregate in this area.

Angling is a popular sport and there are many well-supported clubs throughout the country. Apart from rock and shore angling, the sport is roughly divided by the type of craft used, either the trailer-launched ski-boat (the equivalent of the famed Florida-based blue-water craft), or the larger permanently-moored deep-sea boats.

Game fishing on the east coast is dominated by the ski-boat, with many small towns and villages offering well-patronised launch sites, particularly during the holiday season.

Right *Looking towards Hout Bay, the centre of Cape Town's big-game fishing industry.*

Below *Beach launching from Sodwana Bay on South Africa's northeast coast, near the Mozambique border.*

At Sodwana Bay, just south of the Mozambique border, the challenge of launching through the surf is a prelude to a day's fishing over offshore reefs. This area is famous for its billfish catches and a number of black marlin nearing the magical 454kg (1000 lb) mark have been taken by ski-boats only 5–7m (16–23 ft) in length.

Blue and striped marlin, sailfish, wahoo, king and queen mackerel, barracuda, kingfish and various sharks are found here.

Travelling southward along the coast, the ports of Richards Bay and Durban offer excellent facilities by way of fishing clubs, launch sites and harbours for the larger sportfishing craft, including deep-sea charterboats. Durban is a subtropical city offering top class hotels, restaurants, shopping and sightseeing, warmwater beaches and year-round sunshine.

The 1998 EFSA Game Championships were fished out of Hout Bay, Cape Town. The winning team, from South Africa, shows the result of one day's fishing – a record for the championships.

Continuing southwards to Port Elizabeth and on to Cape Agulhas, the tropical species are replaced by fish that prefer more temperate waters, such as the abundant yellowfin tuna and yellowtail. Black and striped marlin are also encountered in the summer months.

Many popular resort towns and villages along this coast offer launch sites from slipways in harbours or river mouths; but beach launching is less common as the seas are much rougher.

The closest harbours to Cape Agulhas are the picturesque fishing villages of Arniston and Struisbaai, where South Africa's only charter vessel licensed to fish for the great white shark is based. A protected species in South Africa, as in many other countries, it is fished for only on a limited tag and release basis.

More than 100 species of shark are found around South Africa's coast. Many of these are smallish species but the list is still formidable: the bull shark (known locally as the Zambezi shark), various nurse sharks, the ragged-tooth, the great white, shortfin mako, blue, whitetip reef, hammerhead and the tiger shark, to name but a few. One of the most dangerous (because of its very large teeth and powerful jaws) is the bull shark, but fishing boats have been attacked by both great white and mako sharks.

Many ski-boat launch sites are interspersed between these two ports, as well as further south, past the spectacular, untamed Wild Coast of the Transkei to the next major port, East London.

This area is also home to an impressive number of large bottom-feeding species such as the black musselcracker, red steenbras and kabeljou. Endemic to South African waters, and not normally considered big-game species, these fish are strong fighters and are eagerly sought by many local anglers.

Rounding Cape Agulhas one encounters the harbours of Gansbaai and Hermanus before reaching the distinctive headland of Cape Point. Famous for its majestic cliffs, strong seas and gale-force winds, this southern tip of the Cape Peninsula is often incorrectly quoted as being the meeting place of the Atlantic and Indian oceans. To the east of Cape

Point lie the calm, warmer waters of False Bay, served by the harbour at Simon's Town, while to the west is the cold Atlantic. Most local boats fishing the waters off 'the Point' do so from the harbour at Hout Bay, a popular residential suburb on the western side of the Cape Peninsula.

Game fishing craft, including ski-boats operating from Hout Bay, regularly run up to 50 nautical miles offshore from Cape Point during the summer seasonal tuna runs. While Atlantic big-eye and southern bluefin are sometimes caught, the two most common species are the hard-fighting yellowfin, weighing up to 100kg (220 lb) and the abundant longfin tuna, or albacore. The latter grows to record size in the waters of the southwestern Cape and more than 25 world records for longfin tuna have been taken here.

Dense kelp beds and a rocky shoreline mean there are no launch sites between Hout Bay and Cape Town, although there are facilities at Granger Bay, adjacent to the city's harbour and waterfront.

Further along the west coast are the tidal estuary of Langebaan lagoon and the port of Saldanha Bay. This area is dominated by the cold Benguela current and true game fishing is virtually nonexistent, although at times catches of yellowtail and tuna are made offshore, and elf and sharks, including the sporty thresher, can be taken in the estuary. However, there are large commercial fleets fishing the deep waters of the Atlantic for pelagic fish such as pilchard and hake and a significant Cape crayfish (rock lobster) fishery is centred on Saldanha Bay.

Angling is considered to be one of the most popular pastimes in South Africa and more than 9000 registered anglers are members of the South African Deep Sea Angling Association (SADSAA), the body in charge of competitive game fishing. Visiting anglers wishing to make contact with one of the many clubs operating throughout the country, should contact the secretary of SADSAA.

Satour, the country's official tourism organization, will also be able to provide details on the availability of charter fishing anywhere in South Africa.

NAMIBIA

The cold Benguela current sweeps up the coast of Namibia, precluding many of the more conventional big-game fish species, although shore-casting is very popular, particularly around the southern towns of Lüderitz and Swakopmund, where the ochre sands of the Namib desert extend almost to the beach. Deep-sea fishing is done mostly from ski-boats and

many of the operators include day trips into the adjacent Namib desert as part of the package. German is widely spoken in Namibia.

Among the exotic species occurring here are the Namibian coppershark, also called the bronze whaler, which can reach up to 180kg (396 lb), blue stingray, eagle ray and the unusually shaped elephant fish. Snoek, which is caught on hand lines, is a popular eating fish.

KENYA

Kenya is rated as one of the more important game fishing destinations in Africa, with a warm Indian Ocean coastline that stretches for about 550km (342 miles). Blue, striped and black marlin, blacktip shark, various tunas (including yellowfin from August to November), wahoo and sailfish are found in these tropical seas.

The deep waters of the Pemba Channel off Mombasa harbour black, blue and striped marlin and other billfish. The peak fishing time is during the summer months, from November to March. Among the top areas for sailfish are Malindi, a town about 80km (50 miles) north of Mombasa, which has charterboats offering first-class fishing facilities, and Watamu, which is the home of Hemingways, an angling club with legendary status.

Kenya's tourism industry centres on the inland wildlife reserves and many visiting anglers combine big-game fishing with big-game viewing.

The Kenyan record for black marlin stands at 231kg (510 lb), the blue marlin at 567kg (1247 lb), the mako shark at a big 289kg (638 lb) and the hammerhead at 203kg (438 lb).

MOZAMBIQUE

Although Mozambique presents exciting opportunities for anglers who are ready to take on the challenge of towing their boats from South Africa, it is the offshore islands of the Bazaruto Archipelago in the north of the country that offer some of the best angling to be found in this part of the world.

Bazaruto and Benguérua islands offer two resorts each, while the smallest island, Magaruque, has one. The Bazaruto Archipelago has gained a reputation as one of the best spots in the Indian Ocean for black marlin, with several fish over 454kg (1000 lb) taken there in the mid-1970s.

Despite ongoing unrest in parts of the country there are a number of experienced tour and charter companies regularly fishing in these waters.

A sailfish taken by local fishermen off Watamu, Kenya.

Above left *Shore-casting is common along Namibia's desolate Skeleton Coast.*
Above *A good day's fishing on one of the islands in the Bazaruto Archipelago off Mozambique.*

Above *The coral reefs of the Indian Ocean islands form natural feeding grounds for the baitfish on which big-game fish prey.*

Opposite *A well-equipped charterboat sets off for a day's fishing in the Seychelles.*

INDIAN OCEAN ISLANDS

The islands referred to here are individual countries grouped together by geography rather than politics or culture. Their common features are the warm tropical waters in which they are situated and the similarity of the species they offer.

MADAGASCAR

The big-game angler with time and money can fish in South African waters in the southern summer, then travel to this island in May to catch marlin or sailfish, which occur here in large numbers. Although there are a few fishing lodges around the 1600km (944-mile) coastline, the tiny offshore island of Nosy Bé is a new, if rustic, destination to explore.

SEYCHELLES

The Seychelles, a widespread group of 115 islands, is one of the most important game fishing destinations of the Indian Ocean islands.

While berthing and maintenance is available for privately owned boats, the range of boats for hire or charter is impressive. Many of the islands' hotels also have their own well-equipped charterboats.

The Seychelles lie on a shallow continental shelf that surrounds all the main islands. For the best fishing, one needs to be based on one of the more outlying islands, close to the deep waters of the continental drop-off, where the big fish congregate. Fishing interest lies mainly in billfish, including marlin and swordfish, tuna, barracuda and wahoo.

The Seychelles, like other tropical island destinations, is a tourist paradise of white sandy beaches, warm seas and balmy days. A national fishing competition, at which a catch and release policy is implemented, is held each year in April.

REUNION

The French-speaking island of Réunion, which lies to the east of Madagascar, is the site of a still-active volcano. If that isn't enough to deter all but the most adventurous angler, the sharks around Réunion seem to be more prevalent than off the Seychelles or Mauritius – but that may well be sensational hype to make the place sound dangerous.

On the big-game fishing front, there are blue marlin, swordfish and tuna to be found here and the best time for catching game fish is in October.

The names of local professional deep-sea angling syndicates, such as Marlin Club, Pêche au Gros and Blue Marlin, indicate the fishing interest.

MAURITIUS

East of Réunion lies the island of Mauritius, which produces world class fishing for blue marlin between October and February. Each year a few 'granders' – marlin tipping the scales at 454kg (1000 lb) or more – are captured.

Mauritius is a major tourist destination and most of the well-appointed hotels will organize boats for anglers, who can go out for sailfish and blue, black and striped marlin, yellowfin and skipjack tunas, dorado and wahoo. The blue marlin record stands at 648.5kg (1430 lb). There are plenty of sharks too, including mako, hammerhead, tiger, black-fin, white-fin and blue sharks.

Mauritius hosts an annual World Marlin Cup fishing competition, fished out of the capital Port Louis. French is widely spoken here, as it is on most of the Indian Ocean islands.

MALDIVES

Lying north of the equator and situated closer to India than Africa, only 200 of the Maldives' 1200 islands are inhabited.

Highly regarded in scuba diving circles, the Maldives are less well-known for angling, and visitors are advised to ensure that a suitable craft is available at their chosen resort if they intend to go deep-sea fishing, as most of the boats are more suited for divers than anglers.

Yellowfin tuna, sailfish and marlin are found in this part of the Indian Ocean, with weights known to reach over 100kg (220 lb). White-tip reef and hammerhead sharks also occur here.

CAPE VERDE ISLANDS

These remote, windy islands lying 600km off the coast of West Africa are the new hotspot for blue marlin, with up to 10 having been taken by a single boat on one day. Wahoo weighing up to 36kg (80 lb) are also found. Protected anchorage can be found at Mindelo on São Vincente. The offshore reefs harbour baitfish which attract the big-game species.

Left *This fine barracuda was taken off Guinea-Bissau.*

GUINEA-BISSAU

The subtropical Atlantic waters of this West African country hold barracuda, cobia, lemon shark, nurse, blacktip and hammerhead sharks and, it is claimed, the world's heaviest concentration of tiger sharks. The multilingual guides are experts on where and how to catch them and the best time is from October to the beginning of June.

AUSTRALASIA

The big-game fish species normally found in the Pacific and Indian oceans include southern bluefin tuna, black and striped marlin, mako and tiger sharks, among others. Most big-game anglers in Australia and New Zealand support conservation by adopting tag and release fishing methods.

AUSTRALIA

With its vast coastline and the proximity of its major cities to the sea, Australia offers the big-game angler a variety of options, from the cold waters of the south to the warm tropical waters of the north and east coasts. The big-game fish move down the east coast following schools of baitfish that in turn migrate in the warm-water eddies of the East Australian Current, known as the 'River of Life'. This nutrient-rich current originates in the Coral Sea in the far north and flows southward down the east coast as far as Tasmania.

The cool Leewin Current, which originates in the Southern Ocean, flows up the west coast of Australia, also has an abundance of baitfish to attract the big-game species that feed on them.

The most notable geographic feature of the continent is the Great Barrier Reef. which stretches more than 2300km (1400 miles) along the northeast coast of Queensland. While the Barrier Reef is better known as a diving destination, it nevertheless attracts big-game fish that feed on the many reef-dwelling inhabitants. The Great Barrier Reef Marine Park Authority was established in 1975 and the area received World Heritage status in 1981.

Getting out of the city for the weekend is a way of life for many urban Australians, who head for the hills, rivers and sea at every opportunity. Australians enjoy watersports of all kinds and interest in big-game fishing has increased enormously in the past 20 years.

Much of this has been due to the availability of multi-hulled boats in the 5–7m (16–22ft) range. Powered by twin outboard engines, these popular boats can be transported on trailers and are designed to handle a variety of offshore conditions that were once regarded as the sole domain of larger craft. The many harbours and launch sites throughout Australia have helped to promote deep-sea angling as a sport.

New South Wales

The main attraction along the 1900km (1180-mile) coastline of this state is the closeness of the continental shelf and the beneficial effect of the East Australian Current. In many places the shelf is only 16km (10 miles) offshore, within easy reach of smaller boats, ensuring that New South Wales offers excellent big-game fishing opportunities. The East Australian Current, which flows from about December through until June, is often so close to the coast that it licks the headlands of places such as Jervis Bay and Green Cape.

Sydney and its nearby ports of Broken Bay, Botany Bay, Port Hacking and Port Jackson all offer charter facilities. Other popular New South Wales game fishing ports include Coffs Harbour, Port Stephens, Newcastle, Ulladulla, Batemans Bay, Bermagui, Merimbula and Eden. Many of the small coastal towns offer sheltered harbours and protected ramps from which boats can be launched. However some, such as Narooma on the south coast, have sand bars at their entrance that can be dangerous in certain sea conditions.

Yellowfin tuna to 100kg (220 lb) and southern bluefin tuna of similar size are prized captures. There are also northern bluefin (longtail), mackerel and striped tuna along with bonito. Marlin dominate the billfish list, with striped, black and blue marlin all taken; while yellowtail kingfish, cobia, Spanish mackerel, wahoo and mahi mahi (dolphinfish) complete the line-up of big-game fish.

There are also a number of sharks including mako, blue, hammerhead and tiger, as well as several from the lesser-known whale shark family.

In recent years broadbill swordfish have become more sought after. Anglers fish the 1000-fathom line on the far south coast at night, using luminous sticks to attract this, the world's most elusive game fish. Broadbill in excess of 100kg (220 lb) have been boated but much bigger ones have been lost, and anglers hope that it is only a matter of time before a record-breaking specimen is captured.

Live baits, lures, trolled natural baits and cubing methods are all employed in New South Wales.

A game fish tagging programme, initiated by the state, records data on game fish tagged and recaptured throughout Australia. Over 15,000 anglers have been involved in the programme.

Top Marlin, tuna and shark are fished for out of Darwin, in the Northern Territory. **Bottom** *Cairns is considered one of the game-fishing 'capitals' of the world. Queensland has created a thriving tourist industry around the sport.*

Queensland and the Great Barrier Reef

Australia's second largest state is also one of the least populated, with the majority of its inhabitants living in Brisbane and other towns along the Gold Coast and the Sunshine Coast. Queensland has everything in its favour, with a year-round climate that runs from comfortably temperate to tropical.

Tourism, the state's dominant industry, focuses on its 1931km (1200-mile) coastline, specifically on the Great Barrier Reef, which lies between 27–96km (17–60 miles) out to sea.

One of the natural wonders of the world, the 2300km-long (1429-mile) formation is not a continuous reef, but is composed of thousands of small coral communities, making up 2900 individual reefs covering 348,700 km² (128,321 sq. miles). The Great Barrier Reef is a marine biologist's dream, with more than 1500 species of fish, 215 species of bird and six breeding species of turtle occurring here.

Cairns, regarded as the 'sportfishing capital of Australia', has become a big-game fishing centre of international standing and is recognized for its black marlin, with 'granders' – marlin weighing 453.5kg (1000 lb) or more – not at all rare here. Many anglers arrive at Cairns and then transfer to Lizard Island further north, to get closer to the marlin grounds outside the Great Barrier Reef.

A system of mother ships is used to enable anglers to reach those distant parts of the reef that are too far offshore for day trips. Smaller specialized game fishing boats are launched from the mother ships, which provide overnight accommodation, fuel and a general base from which angling and diving operations are conducted.

The marlin season was once thought to run from September through to November, but current thinking is that the species may be there even longer. The Cairns–Lizard Island black marlin fishery was discovered in 1968 and since then more than 9000 marlin have been tagged and released in these waters.

More than 93 percent of billfish caught in Australian waters are tagged and released, rising to 97 percent for black marlin on the Great Barrier Reef. The IGFA lists 14 individual weight records for black marlin taken in this area, including one of 611kg (1347 lb) taken off Lizard Island in 1979. Most marlin are caught on trolled natural baits.

Just about every Queensland seaboard town, and most of the offshore resort islands, offer game fishing. Cooktown, Townsville, Hinchinbrook, Shute Harbour, Gladstone, Hervey Bay, Mooloolabah, Bribie Island, Brisbane and the many towns along the famed Gold Coast all have game fishing facilities.

Among the many species Queenslanders catch, besides marlin, are sailfish, Spanish, school and spotted mackerel, wahoo, yellowfin and northern bluefin (longtail) tuna, cobia, giant trevally and a variety of sharks, including the tiger.

Northern Territory

This thinly populated state has a rugged coastline which is still largely unexplored from an angling perspective. The coastal climate is tropical and divided into two seasons: the Wet, which runs from October to March and the Dry, from April to September. Temperatures seldom drop below the mid-teens on the coast, although in winter in the interior the temperature frequently reaches below freezing at night.

Big-game fishing in the area centres on Darwin, and the angler with plenty of time and money on his hands could well experience the fishing trip of a lifetime by exploring the potential of the Top End – as the untamed northerly parts of the Northern Territory are called. Sailfish, marlin, tuna and sharks are all encountered in these waters.

Western Australia

Keep driving, or sailing, westward past Darwin and you will reach the corrugated edge of the northern part of Western Australia's 6437km (4000 mile) coast. This state offers anglers two challenges: the gigantic scale of the offshore areas (many of which are rarely visited) and the hunt for big-game species. Although much of the northern part of Western Australia's coastline is inaccessible, the more populous southern end of Australia's biggest state has a better infrastructure for anglers.

Broome, which lies north of Eighty Mile Beach, is world famous for its sailfish grounds which produce best from July through to October. The Rowley Shoals offshore from here are a big-game fishing paradise, and black marlin grounds have just been discovered about 80km (50 miles) offshore.

Moving south, the King Sound Game Fishing Club is based at Dampier. Its members fish Rosemary Island and the islands in the Dampier Archipelago for sailfish and other species.

At Exmouth, which is close to the continental shelf, blue, black and striped marlin can still be caught, but the effect of the cool Leewin Current is starting to bring about a change in species. Carnarvon is not very organized as a game fishing port. Nevertheless the locals catch barrel-sized yellowfin tuna near Dorre and Dirk Hartog islands and Steep Point, the most westerly headland in Australia. Land-based game fishermen have also caught sailfish, Spanish mackerel and southern bluefin tuna in this area. Continuing south, the fishing grounds off Geraldton are as yet untapped, although the Abrolhos and Houtman islands are popular destinations for anglers.

Southern bluefin tuna are found off Rottnest Island, near Perth, particularly during the summer months (September to May). The Southern Ocean yields yellowfin tuna, which are fished for out of Albany in the south of the state during the months of April, May and June, while samson fish are caught here from February through to May.

Left *The Great Barrier Reef, one of the natural wonders of the world, can be seen from outer space.*

South Australia

This state offers another long (4059km; 2524-mile) coastline which includes 23 islands and spectacular scenery around Port Lincoln, and the dramatic sheer cliffs and small islands of the Nullarbor Plain and the Great Australian Bight.

Southern bluefin tuna pass close inshore on their seasonal migration from the eastern Indian Ocean to the Pacific and a number of records have been taken from Port Lincoln.

Kangaroo Island, a popular angling destination near Adelaide, lies 48km (30 miles) offshore and can be reached by car ferry. Several great white sharks have been caught from Dangerous Reef, off Kangaroo Island, seven of which went over the tonne, with the heaviest weighing 1192.3kg (2664 lb). These are now a protected species.

Port MacDonnell, in the southeast, is favoured from May to July when the southern bluefin migrate.

Victoria

Tucked between South Australia and New South Wales, the smallest of the mainland states faces the waters of the Southern Ocean and the Tasman Sea. As with South Australia, game fishing opportunities are limited, the majority of it based on sharks,

mainly blues, makos, threshers and bronze whalers, as well as southern bluefin tuna and yellowtail kingfish, which are taken around Portland.

There is not much big-game fishing between Portland and Wilsons Promontory, but some does take place at Western Port and Port Phillip Bay, near Melbourne. Good catches of yellowtail kingfish have declined in this area, leaving just sharks and sometimes southern bluefin. Charterboats out of Port Albert and Port Welshpool target mainly yellowtail kingfish and shark but sometimes find yellowfin and southern bluefin tuna. Mallacoota Inlet and Gabo Island have access to marlin, yellowfin and yellowtail kingfish grounds in the Tasman Sea.

Tasmania

Although Australia's smallest state is a trout-fisherman's paradise, big-game anglers will find that they are well catered for, particularly on the east coast, from Anson's Bay to Bicheno, with St Helens the major port for game fishing.

During the summer months when the East Australian Current flows past, the Tasman Sea has southern bluefin and yellowfin tuna, albacore and black and striped marlin. In some seasons the current is less than 8km (5 miles) offshore, making it easily accessible for small craft.

NEW ZEALAND

New Zealand, separated from Australia by the Tasman Sea, is made up of the North Island, the South Island, Stewart Island and a number of smaller islands. No matter where one is based in New Zealand, the sea is a mere few hours away – a huge boon for the big-game angler.

Game fishing in New Zealand came to the fore in February 1915, when the first big-game fish caught on rod and reel in these waters – a striped marlin weighing 101kg (223 lb) – was taken from the Bay of Islands. Zane Grey (by then a noted angler), travelled from his home in Ohio, USA, at the request of the New Zealand government, to assess the state of the fishing. His success in locating big-game fish resulted in New Zealand being put on the big-game fishing map with a vengeance.

New Zealand has a thriving sportfishing industry because overfishing by commercial interests and the consequent dwindling of stocks has not occurred

NEW ZEALAND BIG GAME FISHING COUNCIL

Over the last 80 years or so, big-game fishing in New Zealand has flourished.

In 1957 the New Zealand Big Game Fishing Council was set up to provide a means of amicable communication between the various sea-angling clubs and at the same time enforce good angling standards. Today, it looks after the interests of some 25,000 keen big-game anglers in 39 fishing clubs and societies throughout the country.

The Fishing Council supports and promotes ethical and sustainable fishing practices, including tag and release programmes for big-game fish.

All claims for record fish in the various line classes must be ratified by the IGFA.

New Zealand Big Game Fishing Council, PO Box 567, Whangarei, New Zealand.

here to the extent it has elsewhere. New Zealand anglers also support tag and release programmes.

There are 400 fish species around New Zealand's 6437km (4000-mile) coastline, a fifth of which are found nowhere else. All the big-game species occur here, but it is the striped marlin which is the most common big-game fish in these waters, with an average weight of 155kg (342 lb). Other species include black and blue marlin; mako, hammerhead, blue, thresher, whaler and tiger sharks; yellowfin, big-eye and southern bluefin tuna, and albacore.

The North Island

The Bay of Islands, on the northeast coast of the North Island, regarded as having some of the best marlin fishing in the world, was described as an 'angler's El Dorado' by Zane Grey.

The 144 islands that make up the Bay of Islands Maritime Park offer every kind of big-game fishing, including blue, striped and black marlin, broadbill, yellowfin tuna, yellowtail, and mako, hammerhead and thresher sharks. A number of world records, particularly for striped marlin, come from this area, which is also renowned for oysters and crayfish.

The South Island

The rocky coast of the South Island makes boat launching difficult and, coupled with the colder seas in the south, this means that New Zealand's main big-game fishing centres are found off the North Island.

PAPUA NEW GUINEA

About a hundred miles off northern Australia lies Papua New Guinea. Anglers prepared to rough it might fancy travelling to this part of the world in search of marlin (the marlin potential is said to match that of Cairns), sailfish, dog-tooth tuna and billfish. Boats can be hired at Port Moresby and Rabaul, but prebooking is essential.

Above *A fine haul of yellowfin tuna from St Helens, Tasmania.* **Opposite** *A ski boat punches through the waves off Victoria.* **Left** *New Zealand's extensive coastline offers some excellent big-game fishing as well as spectacular scenery.*

GLOSSARY

Anti-kink vane Having a keel and made of lead or plastic, the anti-kink vane can be mounted behind the swivel to prevent the line from becoming twisted as the swivel turns.

Backing Some reel drums (spools) take a great deal of line and in order to avoid the expense of purchasing several hundred metres of line that is not likely to be used, a line of much larger diameter is first wound on, taking up more room than line of a finer diameter.

Blank Rod sections made of any of the man-made materials, glass fibre, carbon fibre or Kevlar, prior to the attachment of ferrules, spigots, rings or the butt section.

Braided line Monofilament line that is woven into a stronger, multistrand line. The breaking strain is multiplied by the number of woven strands.

Breaking strain Usually just B.S.or b.s., this is the technically assessed pull in metric or imperial measures at which the line breaks when dry.

Butt The base of a fishing rod, having a grip, originally of cork, but other materials have since taken over.

Carbon fibre A thread of pure fibre whose properties are strength and lightness. Used in rod manufacture.

Caudal fin The tail fin of a fish.

Centre-pin reel Fishing reel, with the spool parallel to the rod, where line is retrieved by turning the handle.

Cephalopoda A class of molluscs that includes the cuttlefish, squid, octopus and the rarely seen nautilus.

Charterboat Skippered by professional crews, charterboats can be hired for varying periods. Equipment includes fishing gear, baits, electronic fishfinders, short-wave radio, navigational equipment and first aid

Chum Mashed or chopped fish pieces, often mixed with other ingredients, fed over the side to form a slick to attract predatory fish.

Clutch This mechanism allows the angler to free the drum from the winding handle so that the reel can revolve freely. Clutch plates apply pressure on the fish and prevent the line from being broken.

Continental shelf The comparatively shallow water bordering the continents and extending to varying distances from the shore.

Dorsal fin The back fin of a fish. Maintains balance when swimming.

Drift fishing Fishing on or close to the bottom with the baited hook sunk to a predetermined depth by a suitable weight. Speed of tide and current will dictate the weight required.

Echo-sounder Navigation and position-finding device that sends a pulse down to the seabed, from which it bounces back, the time delay being converted into a depth reading.

Fathom A unit of measure. One fathom equals 1.8 metres (6ft).

Ferrules Ideally, rods should be of one continuous construction, but for ease of transport the sections are joined by metal ferrules in which the upper section sits in the female section to form as near a perfect fit as possible. Metal ferrules affect the flexibility of the joined rod sections. (*See also* Spigots.)

Fibreglass A trade name for glass fibre, an early rod material which was solid and strong, but heavy. Hollowglass, devised by wrapping material round a mould and spraying it with synthetic resin, proved much lighter, but under pressure rods made from it had a tendency to buckle and fold.

Fixed-spool reel A reel that has the spool at right-angles to the rod and where line is recovered by a revolving arm, or freed by the arm being hinged up and back so that the line pulls off freely. (*See also* Centre-pin reel.)

Flotsam Material or cargo lost overboard which remains on the surface. The difference between flotsam and jetsam is a legal quibble, jetsam being that which has been thrown overboard, not 'lost'.

Flying gaff A gaff with a head which pulls free of the handle and leaves the gaffed fish attached to the boat by a strong chain and length of rope.

Food chain The natural system of microscopic organisms being eaten by larger ones, which are taken by small fish. These are eaten by larger fish, which when they die decompose to form the nutrients for microscopic life, and so the cycle begins again.

Foodfish Any smaller fish which is eaten by another, larger fish.

Gaff A stout pole with a large, strong hook used to lift heavy or dangerous fish from the sea. The gaff should never be used if the fish is to be released. (*See also* Flying gaff).

Gear ratio Fixed-spool reels and multiplier reels have a gear system that provides a determined number of turns of the drum to one turn of the handle; given as 1:5, 1:10 and so on.

Gill The means whereby fish extract oxygen from the water. The gills are protected by gill-covers, correctly named *operculae* (singular *operculum*).

Grapnel A hook used to hold a boat over rough ground or rocks, when an ordinary anchor might be difficult to dislodge. The points of a grapnel are malleable enough to be pulled straight, freeing the anchorage.

Greenheart Flexible, attractive dense wood used, together with bamboo, for fishing rods before man-made materials were devised. Greenheart had the tendency to split unexpectedly.

Hollowglass *See* Fibreglass.

Hooks A hook has a number of features: eye, shank, bend, throat, barb, point. The shank runs from the eye down to the bend, the inside of which is the throat. The barb is cut on the inside near to the point. If the barb is cut too deep this constitutes a weak link in the hook. Points can be twisted sideways, kirbed, reversed, upturned (Dublin or superior), downturned (hollow), or given a sharpened edge.

Intelligence Whatever impression they may give, fish have no intelligence as we know it. The largest fish brain, relative to body-size, is that of the freshwater carp, *Cyprinus carpio*, the intelligence of which has been assessed as that of a domestic chicken.

Lateral line A usually visible line of sensory cells running along the flanks of fish and reptiles and extending to a complex pattern on the head. Part of the nervous system, these cells detect changes of pressure, vibrations and low-pitched sounds in the water surrounding the animal.

Level-wind A most useful device on multiplier reels that carries the recovered line across the drum or spool and distributes it evenly to avoid bunching.

Mark A known place where fish have been caught regularly, fixed visually when close inshore, or by satellite coordinates or navigating to a specific point on a chart.

Metal rods At the end of World War II the radio aerials of armoured vehicles were found to make reasonable fishing rods. This led to aluminium-rods being manufactured, but after lighter and more flexible man-made materials were devised, metal rods ceased being used.

Monofilament Single-strand man-made filament line manufactured in breaking strains from 113g (4oz) to 60kg (130 lb).

Multiplier reels As the name suggests, the multiplier gives a set number of turns of the drum to one of the handle. Different ratios are available. The reel is fitted on top of the rod and has a a clutch, which is disengaged when casting.

Nematocyst The stinging organs of jellyfish and sea anemones, comprising a sharp thread linked to a poison sac which shoots out when touched. Lethal to small fish, they produce a painful wound in human flesh.

Outrigger Pole that extends from the side of a boat. In angling terms, these allow four or five lines to be employed as the boat trolls. Clips hold the lines until a strike occurs. When the boat is berthed, the outriggers fold back.

Pectoral fins Paired fins attached to the bony body wall of a fish, that help to control the direction of movement.

Pelagic Fish species living in, or close to, the surface layers of the open sea.

Pelvic fins Situated usually behind the pectoral fins, the pelvic fins of a fish aid stability in the water.

Pirk A weighted, brightly coloured artificial lure, fished by up-and-down movements of the rod.

Plug An artificial lure, sometimes jointed and designed to imitate the movements of a small fish, usually carrying a single treble hook.

Polarised glasses Extremely useful glasses with lenses that filter out surface glare and reflections, enabling the wearer to see through the surface layer. Polaroid is a trade name.

Shoal A group of fish, not always of the same species but moving together. Also called a 'school'.

Spigots Brass ferrules (*see also Ferrules*) were not the most problem-free method of joining rod sections, so spigots were devised. Using the same material as the rod, the ends of the rod sections are formed as male and female joints and give more flexibility to the complete rod.

Spoon Artificial lures that flutter but do not spin and thus provide different vibrations in the water.

Tackle The term covers everything that the angler has with him in order to carry out his/her fishing exercise.

Taxonomy The science of classifying organisms into groups based on similarities of structure, origin etc., usually of the animal world. From the Greek *taxis* (law) and *nomy* (to govern).

Terminal tackle The rig or trace attached to the end of the line including all swivels, lures or baited hooks.

Test curve If a fishing rod is held horizontally and a weight attached to the tip, the test curve is the weight needed to bring the tip to the vertical. With heavy duty rods this can be a negative assessment, the weight necessary being greater than any angler would be prepared to lower to the seabed and recover with a heavy, struggling fish as added weight.

Trolling The action of towing a lure or baited hook behind a moving boat to attract a feeding fish. Specialized trolling rods are used for stand-up and conventional trolling techniques.

CONVERSION CHART		
FROM	TO	MULTIPLY BY
Metres	feet	3.28
Feet	metres	0.305
Kilometres	miles	0.621
Miles	kilometres	1.61
Kilograms	pounds	2.20
Pounds	kilograms	0.454
Litres	pints	1.76
Pints	litres	0.568

To convert Celsius to Fahrenheit:
x 9 ÷ 5 + 32

INDEX

CONTACT INFORMATION

It would be impossible to provide a comprehensive list of contact names for angling associations and charter companies worldwide. The following is only a fraction of the many organisations that exist to promote and participate in the sport of big-game fishing. Your local angling club or travel agent should be able to assist with further details. All information was correct at the time of going to print.

Australia

John Harrison, executive director

Recfish Australia

PO Box 854, Dickson ACT 2602 Australia

Tel: +61 2 6257-1977 Fax: +61 2 6247-9314

www.gfaa.asn.au/

Terry Parker Charters (Brisbane and Cairns)

93 Glenmount Rd, Buderim QLD 4556

Tel/Fax: +61 7 54477 0014

Bahamas

Treasure Cay Resort Hotel and Marina

Tel: + 1242 365-8250 Fax: +1242 365-8847

e-mail: abaco@gate.net

Bermuda

Bermuda Sportfishing Association

Creek View House, 8 Tulo Lane, Pembroke

HM02. Tel: +1441 295-2307

England

David Styles,, Secretary, EFSA England

12 Woodhouse Road, Hove, East Sussex BN3 5NE, England.

Tel/Fax: +44 (1273) 88-1092

Gibraltar

J. Lara. Secretary, EFSA Gibraltar

8 Schomberg, South Barrack Road, Gibraltar.

Tel: +350 75-444

Hawaii

Peter S. Fithian, chairman

Hawaiian International Billfish Association

PO Box 4800 Kailua-Kona, HI 96745 USA

Tel: +1 808 329-6155 Fax: +1 808 329-1148

http://www.holoholo/org/billfish

Madeira

Captain Peter Bristow, Quintas das Malvas, Rua da Levada da Santa Luzia 124, 9050 Funchal, Madeira, Portugal

Tel: +351 91 22-0334 Fax: +351 91 22-9896

e-mail: p-bristow@usa.net

Malta

Alfred Bugeja, Secretary, EFSA Malta

Almar, Triq Salvu Bonnano, Monterosa Gardens, San Gwann SGN 10, Malta.

Tel: +356 37-6575

Mauritius

Mr J. Maurice de Speville

Striker Big Game Fishing

La Preneuse, Black River, Mauritius

Tel: +230 683-6387 Fax: +230 683-6386

Mexico

Los Cabos Reel Sportfishing, Los Cabos Marina, Los Cabos, Baja California, Mexico

e-mail: Gerry@sportfishingcabo.com

Pisces Fleet - Attn: Marco Ehrenberg

Tel: +52 114 31288 Fax: +52 114 30588

e-mail: 104 164.1105@compuserve.com

New Zealand

New Zealand Big Game Fishing Council

PO Box 93, Whangarei, New Zealand.

Tel: +64 9 437-3791 Fax: +64 9 437-3721

e-mail: nzbgfc@ihug.co.nz

Seychelles

Martin and Anna Lewis, Game Fishing Enterprises (Tam Tam Charters)

PO Box 134, Victoria, Mahe, Seychelles

Tel/Fax: +248 344266

e-mail: bestof@seychelles.net

South Africa

Hymie Steyn, Public relations officer

South African Deep Sea Angling Association

PO Box 4191 Cape Town 8000 South Africa

Tel/Fax: +27 21 964454

United States

International Game Fish Association

300 Gulf Stream Way, Dania Beach, Florida 33004 USA

Tel: +1 954 927-2628 Fax: +1 954 924-4299

e-mail: IGFAHQ@aol.com

PUBLISHER'S ACKNOWLEDGEMENTS

The publisher would like to thank the Sampo Division of the Rome Speciality Company, Barneveld, New York; the SM Group (Europe) Ltd; Eagle UK, of Plymouth, Devon, makers of fish finders and GPS receivers; Everol, of Salvatore, Italy, makers since 1958 of extremely fine big-game reels; St. Croix of Park Falls, WI, USA, makers of high-quality rods; Seven Strand of Long Beach, California; Tournament Tackle Inc., of Satellite Beach, California; Nic de Kock of Tinker Lures, Hout Bay, Cape Town; and Keith Tait of Peg Leg's Place, Salt River, Cape Town; for their assistance with information on tackle and equipment. Also to Vaughan Humphrey and Uwe Schmitt, owner and skipper of 'Sensation', based in Hout Bay, Cape Town, for generously offering both expertise and their magnificent boat for photographic sessions. Many others have given of their time and advice, among them Jeanne Renick of the International Game Fish Association; Robert C Dinsdale, records officer of the New Zealand Big Game Fishing Council; and Hamish R Holmes, honorary general secretary of the European Federation of Sea Anglers.

PHOTOGRAPHIC CREDITS

Ardea/JE Swedberg: p20 (left); **Ardea/Francois Gohier:** p20 (top); **Ardea/Benn Cropp:** pp26–27; **Ardea/Ron and Valerie Taylor:** pp 19, 49; **Ardea/Becca Saunders:** p50; **Ardea/P. Morris:** p61 (bottom left), **Ardea/Piers Cavendish:** p147 (top); **J. Ashley:** cover, pp29, 74, 75 (top left), 76, 81 (top right), 84 (right), 91; **Bios/Seitre:** p23; **Bios/Michel Gunther:** p59 (top left); **G. Booth:** pp38, 41, 56 (top left), 57 (top), 75 (bottom), 97 (top), 102 (top & bottom left); **J. Allan Cash:** pp60 (bottom), 61 (bottom right); **Christel Clear:** cover (spine), back cover (top left), pp12 (top), 13 (right), 15, 16 (top), 56 (centre), 57 (left), 70, 72 (top & bottom), 73 (centre & bottom), 79 (bottom), 81 (bottom right & left), 82 (bottom left), 84 (top left, centre left & bottom left), 85, 87 (left), 102 (bottom right), 103 (left), 104; **Bruce Coleman Limited/Charles & Sandra Hood:** pp46, 52, 58; **Bruce Coleman Limited/Quentin M. Bennett:** p55; **Bruce Coleman Limited/Jeff Foott Productions:** p61 (centre); **Nic de Kock:** p145 (right); **Jean du Plessis:** pp140–141, 146, 155 (bottom); **Getty Images South Africa/Nigel Snowdon:** p126; **Getty Images South Africa/Chad Ehlers:** p127; **Getty Images South Africa/Lou Avers:** p131; **Getty Images South Africa/Hugh Sitton:** p138; **Getty Images South Africa/Oliver Strewe:** endpapers; **Trevor Housby:** pp24, 25 (top), 59 (bottom & top right); **Rick Huckstepp:** pp7, 10–11, 31, 37, 56 (bottom left, centre & near right), 103 (top right & bottom right), 128–129; **Mike Millman:** cover (back flap, bottom), pp14, 21, 53 (bottom right), 60 (left), 61 (top right), 66, 122, 135; **John Neubauer:** pp113, 119; **New Holland Image Library/Anthony Johnson:** p150 (top & bottom); **Charles Norman:** pp 4, 56 (bottom far right), 73 (top), 80, 97 (bottom); **Julian Pepperell:** p71; **Photo Access-Getaway/David Steele:** pp32, 72 (centre), 144; **Photo Access/Dennis Hallinan:** p107; **Photo Access/Dennie Cody:** p114; **Photo Access/Ron Chapple:** pp115, 123; **Photo Access/James Blank:** p116 (left); **Photo Access-Photo Source/E. Nagele:** p116 (bottom); **Photo Access/Bill Losh:** p117; **Photo Access/Dick Luria:** p118; **Photo Access/Don Hebert:** pp120, 121, 124; **Photo Access/Roger Antrobus:** p134; **Photo Access/Walter Knirr:** p145 (left); **Photo Access-Getaway/D. Rogers:** p147 (bottom); **Photo Access-Getaway/Patrick Wagner:** pp148, 149 (bottom); **Photo Access-Photo Source/CLB:** p152; **Graeme Pullen/Fishpix:** pp132, 133 (left & right), 137, 149 (top), 154, 155 (top); **Mariëlle Renssen:** p13; **Struik Image Library/Shaen Adey:** p143; **Struik Image Library/Kelly Walsh:** cover (front flap bottom, back flap top, spine top), pp1, 2–3, 5, 9, 25 (centre top, centre middle & bottom), 52 (bottom left), 53 (top right), 54 (top), 57 (right), 62, 63, 64, 65, 67, 68–69, 75 (top right), 77 (top, centre & bottom), 78 (left and right), 79 (top), 82 (top left & right), 86, 87 (right), 88–89, 93, 94 (top & bottom left), 95, 96, 98, 99, 100, 101, 105, 106.